BASICS OF KEYBOARD THEORY

LEVEL 4

Seventh Edition

Julie McIntosh Johnson

J. Johnson Music Publications
P.O. Box 230
Lockwood, CA 93932
Phone: (714) 961-0257
Fax: (714) 242-9350
www.bktmusic.com
info@bktmusic.com

Basics of Keyboard Theory Level 4, Seventh Edition

Published by:

J. Johnson Music Publications
P.O. Box 230
Lockwood, CA 93932
(714) 961-0257
www.bktmusic.com

Library of Congress Cataloging in Publication Data

Johnson, Julie Anne McIntosh
Basics of Keyboard Theory, Level 4, Seventh Edition

ISBN 10 - 1-891757-32-6
ISBN 13 - 978-1-891757-32-7

LC TX 3 431 937

TO THE TEACHER

Intended as a supplement to private or group music lessons, *Basics of Keyboard Theory Level 4* presents basic theory concepts to the intermediate music student. This level is to be used with the student who has had approximately 4-5 years of music lessons, and is playing piano literature at the level of Schumann's *The Merry Farmer* or Burgmüller's *Ballade.*

Basics of Keyboard Theory, Level 4 is divided into 16 lessons, plus two reviews and a practice test. Application of theory concepts is made to piano music of the student's level. Lessons may be combined with one another or divided into smaller sections, depending on the ability of the student. Whenever possible, it is helpful to demonstrate theory concepts on the keyboard and apply them to the music the student is playing.

Learning music theory can be a very rewarding experience for the student when carefully applied to lessons. *Basics of Keyboard Theory, Level 4*, is an important part of learning this valuable subject.

TABLE OF CONTENTS

Basics of Keyboard Theory is dedicated to my husband Rob,
without whose love, support, help, and patience,
this series would not have been possible.

LESSON 1
MAJOR KEY SIGNATURES

The **KEY SIGNATURE** for a composition is found at the beginning of the music between the clef and the time signature.

The **KEY SIGNATURE** indicates two things:

1. The key or tonality of the music.

2. Which notes will receive sharps or flats.

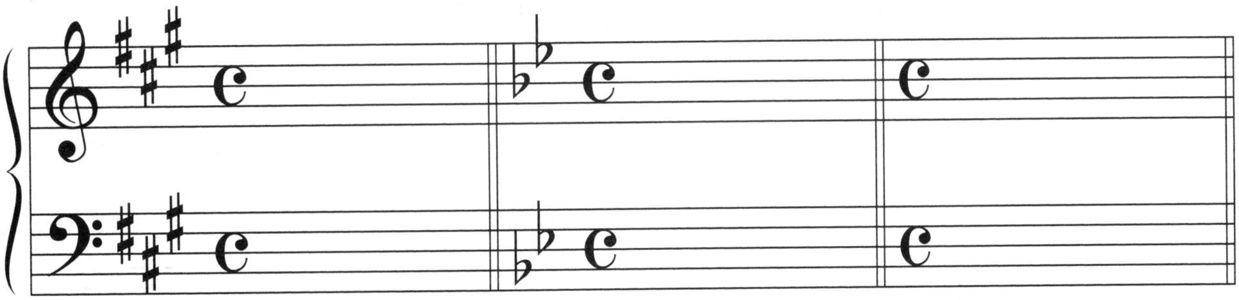

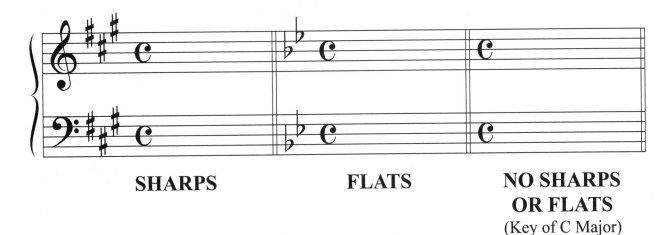

SHARPS **FLATS** **NO SHARPS OR FLATS** (Key of C Major)

If a key signature has sharps, they will be in this order on these lines and spaces. This is called the **ORDER OF SHARPS**.

A saying to help remember this order is:

Fat Cats Go Down Alleys Eating Bologna

If you find errors in this book, please email info@bktmusic.com. Corrections are posted at www.bktmusic.com.

If a key signature has one sharp, it will be F♯. If a key signature has two sharps, they will be F♯ and C♯, etc.

1. Fill in the blanks.

   a. If a key signature has two sharps, they will be F and C.

   b. If a key signature has three sharps, they will be F, C, and G.

   c. If a key signature has one sharp, it will be F.

   d. If a key signature has six sharps, they will be F, C, G, D, A, and E.

2. Draw the Order of Sharps three times in both clefs.

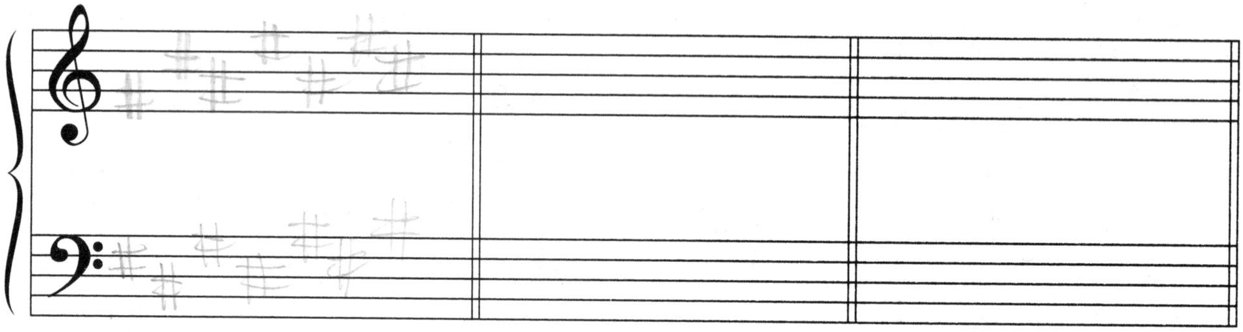

To determine which Major key a group of sharps represents, find and name the last sharp (the sharp furthest to the right), then go up a half step. The note which is a half step above the last sharp is the name of the Major key.

Three sharps: F♯, C♯, G♯

Last sharp is G♯

A half step above G♯ is A

Key of A Major

3. Name these Major keys.

a.

1. The sharps are F, G, G.

2. The last sharp is G.

3. A half step above this sharp is A.

4. Key of A Major.

b.

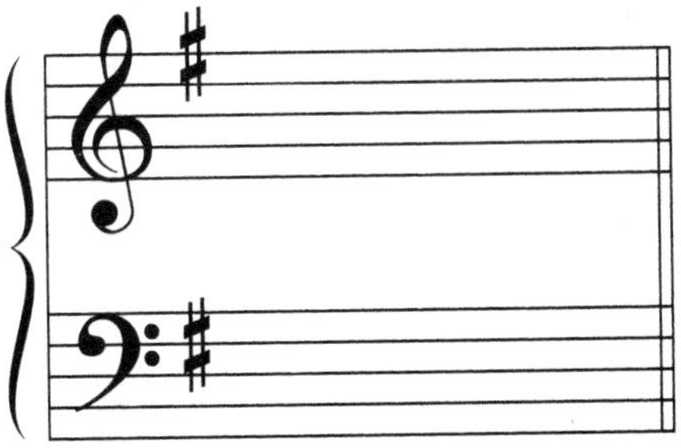

1. The sharp is F.

2. The last sharp is F.

3. A half step above this sharp is G.

4. Key of G Major.

c.

1. The sharps are F, C, G, D, A.

2. The last sharp is A.

3. A half step above this sharp is B.

4. Key of B Major.

d.

1. The sharps are F, C, G, D.

2. The last sharp is D.

3. A half step above this sharp is E.

4. Key of E Major.

e. 

1. The sharps are F, C, G, D, A, E.
2. The last sharp is E.
3. A half step above this sharp is F#.
4. Key of F# Major.

f. 

1. The sharps are F, C, G, D, A, E, B.
2. The last sharp is B.
3. A half step above this sharp is C#.
4. Key of C# Major.

g. 

1. The sharps are F, C.
2. The last sharp is C.
3. A half step above this sharp is D.
4. Key of D Major.

To determine which sharps are in a Major key, find the sharp which is a half step below the name of the key. Name all the sharps from the Order of Sharps up to and including that sharp.

Key of D Major

A half step below D is C#

Name all sharps, from the order of sharps, up to and including C#

F# and C#

4. Fill in the blanks and draw the key signatures for these keys in both clefs.

a. Key of B Major

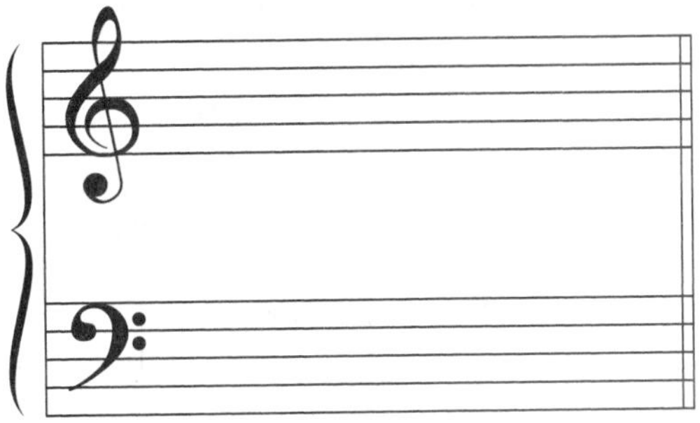

1. A half step below B is A#.
2. The Order of Sharps up to this sharp is F, C, G, D, A.
3. Draw the sharps on the staff in both clefs.

b. Key of G Major

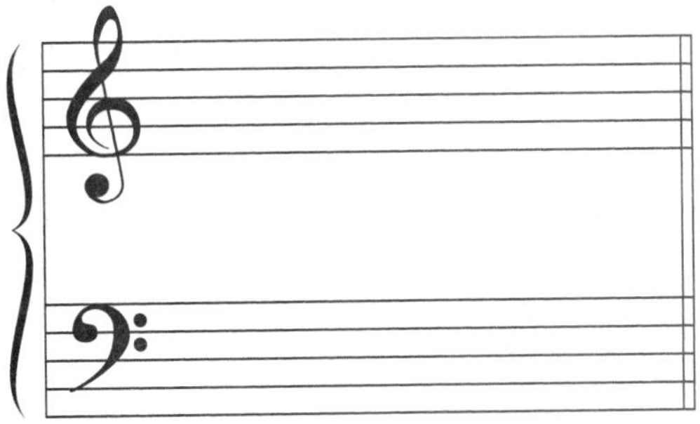

1. A half step below G is F#.
2. The Order of Sharps up to this sharp is F.
3. Draw the sharps on the staff in both clefs.

c. Key of D Major

1. A half step below D is C#.
2. The Order of Sharps up to this sharp is F, C.
3. Draw the sharps on the staff in both clefs.

d. Key of E Major

1. A half step below E is D#.
2. The Order of Sharps up to this sharp is F, C, G, D.
3. Draw the sharps on the staff in both clefs.

e. Key of A Major

1. A half step below A is G#.
2. The Order of Sharps up to this sharp is F, C, G.
3. Draw the sharps on the staff in both clefs.

f. Key of C♯ Major

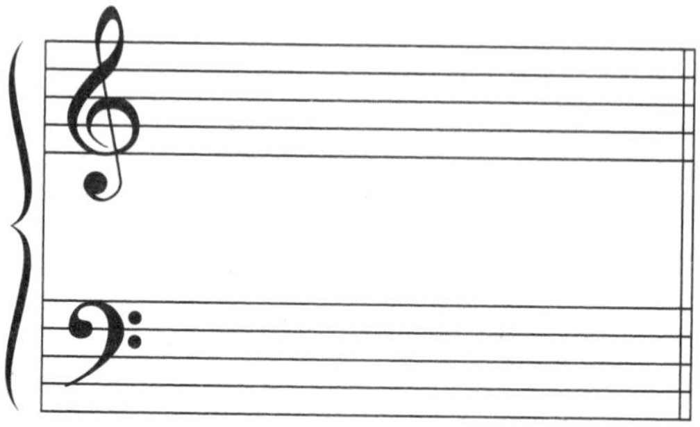

1. A half step below C♯ is C.
2. The Order of Sharps up to this sharp is F, C, G, D, A, E, B.
3. Draw the sharps on the staff in both clefs.

g. Key of F♯ Major

1. A half step below F♯ is F.
2. The Order of Sharps up to this sharp is F, C, G, D, A, E.
3. Draw the sharps on the staff in both clefs.

5. Match these key signatures with their names by drawing lines to connect them.

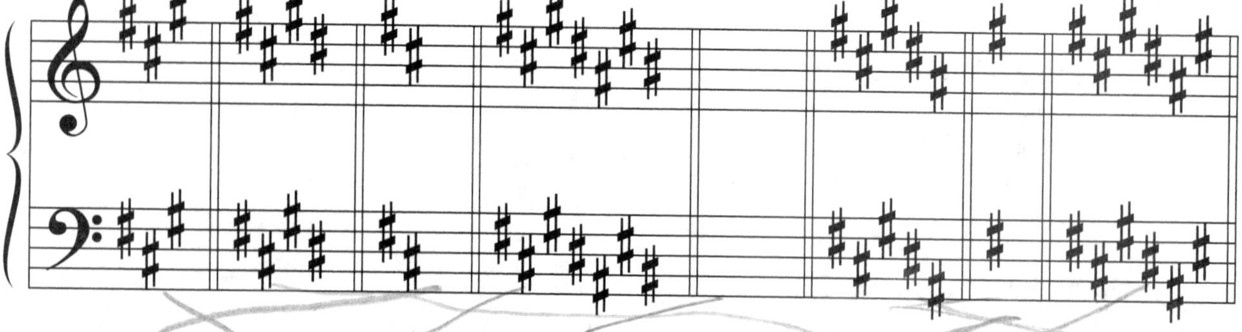

D Major A Major C♯ Major C Major G Major E Major F♯ Major B Major

6. Memorize these key signatures.

C Major	No sharps or flats
G Major	F♯
D Major	F♯ C♯
A Major	F♯ C♯ G♯
E Major	F♯ C♯ G♯ D♯
B Major	F♯ C♯ G♯ D♯ A♯
F♯ Major	F♯ C♯ G♯ D♯ A♯ E♯
C♯ Major	F♯ C♯ G♯ D♯ A♯ E♯ B♯

If a key signature has flats, they will be in this order on these lines and spaces. This is called the **ORDER OF FLATS.**

THE ORDER OF FLATS

The Order of Flats can be memorized with this saying: **BEAD, Gum, Candy, Fruit**

If a key signature has one flat, it will be B♭. If it has two flats, they will be B♭ and E♭, etc.

7. Fill in the blanks.

a. If a key signature has two flats, they are __B__ and __E__.

b. If a key signature has four flats, they are __B__, __E__, __A__, and __D__.

c. If a key signature has three flats, they are __B__, __E__, and __A__.

d. If a key signature has one flat, it is __B__.

8. Draw the Order of Flats three times in both clefs.

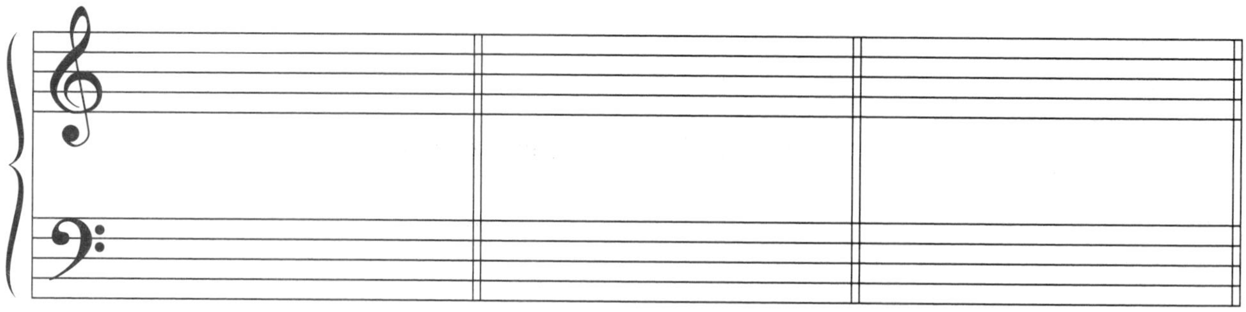

To determine which Major key a group of flats represents, name the next to last flat.

Three flats: B♭, E♭, A♭

Next to last flat is E♭

Key of E♭ Major

The key signature for F Major is an exception. It has one flat: B♭.

KEY SIGNATURE FOR F MAJOR

9. Name these Major keys.

a. 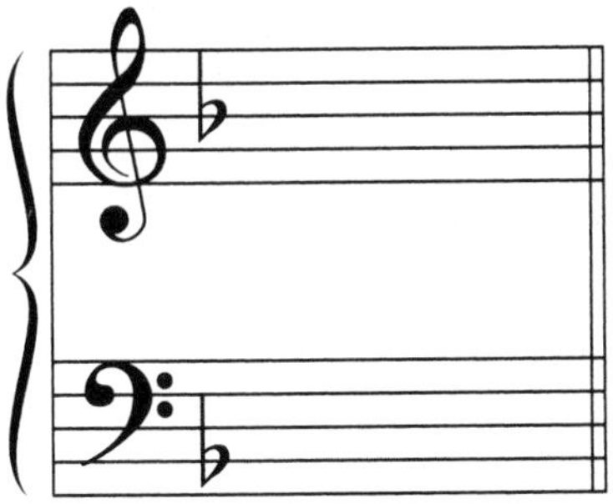

1. One flat: B.

2. This key signature must be memorized.

3. Key of F Major.

b. 

1. Two flats: B and E.

2. Next to last flat is B.

3. Key of Bb Major.

c. 

1. Four flats: B, E, A, D.

2. Next to last flat is A.

3. Key of Ab Major.

d. 

1. Five flats: B, E, A, D, G.

2. Next to last flat is: D.

3. Key of Db Major.

e.

1. Seven flats: B, E, A, D, G, C, F.

2. Next to last flat is C.

3. Key of C♭ Major.

f.

1. Six flats: B, E, A, D, G, C.

2. Next to last flat is G.

3. Key of G♭ Major.

g.

1. Three flats: B, E, A.

2. Next to last flat is E.

3. Key of E♭ Major.

To determine which flats are needed for a Major key, name all the flats from the Order of Flats up to and including the name of the key, then add one more.

Key of E♭ Major

Name all flats from the Order of Flats up to and including E♭, then add one more

B♭, E♭, A♭

10. Write the key signatures for these keys.

a. Key of B♭ Major

Name all flats from the Order of Flats up to and including B♭, then add one more.

B, E

b. Key of E♭ Major

Name all flats from the Order of Flats up to and including E♭, then add one more.

B, E, A

c. Key of D♭ Major

Name all flats from the Order of Flats up to and including D♭, then add one more.

B, E, A, D, G

d. Key of G♭ Major

Name all flats from the Order of Flats up to and including G♭, then add one more.

B, E, A, D, G, C

e. Key of C♭ Major

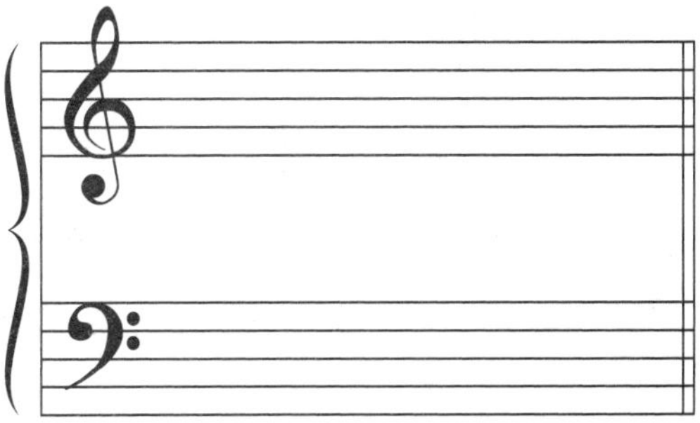

Name all flats from the Order of Flats up to and including C♭, then add one more.

B, E, A, D, G, C, F

f. Key of F Major

Memorize this key signature.

B

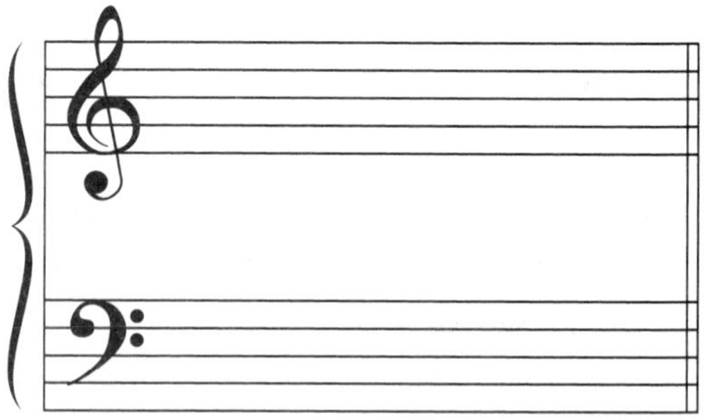

g. Key of A♭ Major

Name all flats from the Order of Flats up to and including A♭, then add one more.

B, E, A, D

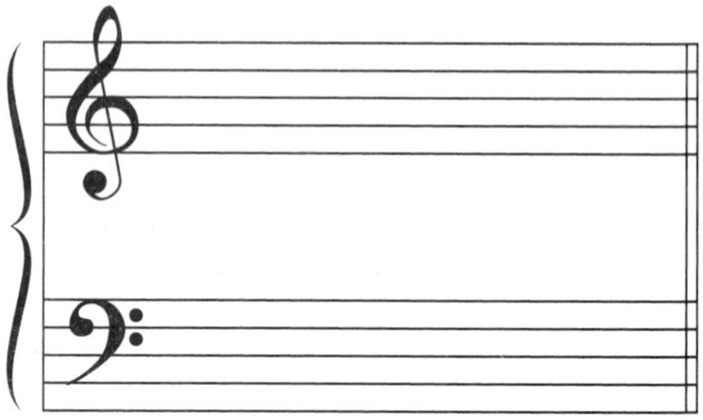

11. Match these key signatures with their names by drawing lines to connect them.

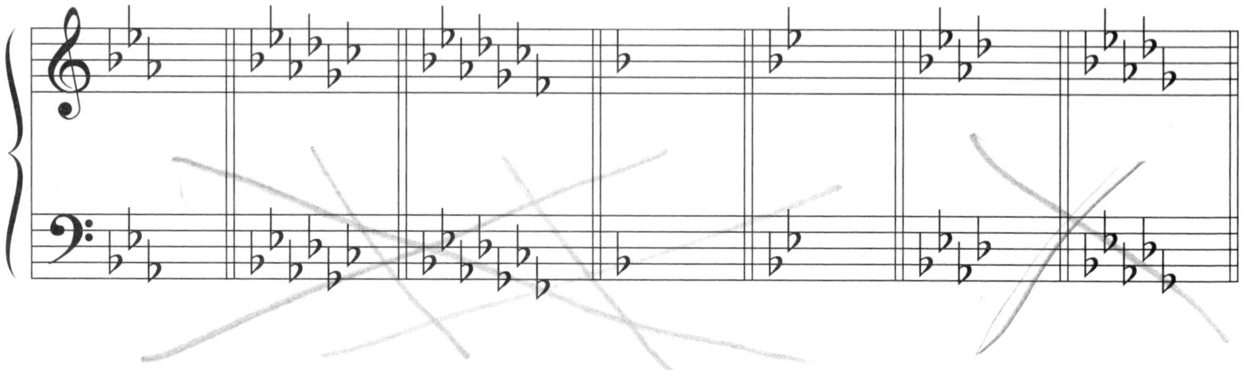

F Major   B♭ Major   G♭ Major   C♭ Major   E♭ Major   D♭ Major   A♭ Major

12. Memorize these key signatures.

F Major	B♭
B♭ Major	B♭ E♭
E♭ Major	B♭ E♭ A♭
A♭ Major	B♭ E♭ A♭ D♭
D♭ Major	B♭ E♭ A♭ D♭ G♭
G♭ Major	B♭ E♭ A♭ D♭ G♭ C♭
C♭ Major	B♭ E♭ A♭ D♭ G♭ C♭ F♭

LESSON 2
MAJOR SCALES

A **SCALE** is an organized sequence of notes upon which the music is based.

MAJOR SCALES have eight notes that are each a step apart. They begin and end with notes of the same letter name, and have all the sharps or flats from the key signature with the same name.

Example: D Major Scale begins and ends on D and has F♯ and C♯.

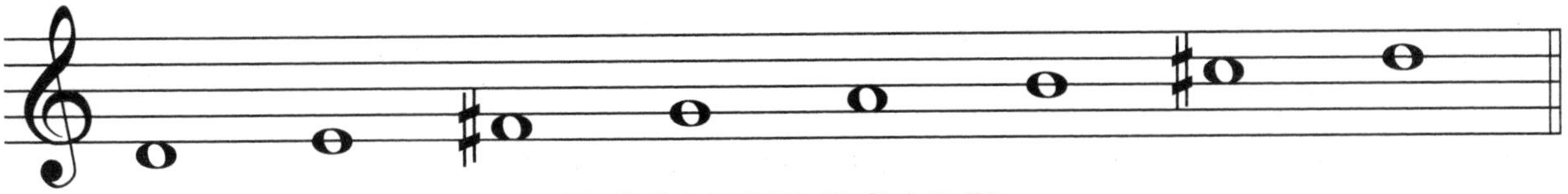

D MAJOR SCALE

1. Determine the key signature for each of the following scales. Draw the sharps or flats from the key signature before the notes to complete each scale. If the scale begins with a sharp or flat, it ends with a sharp or flat. The first one is given.

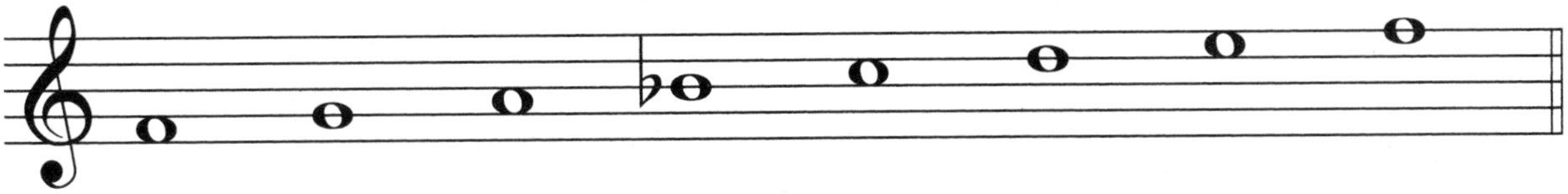

F Major Scale

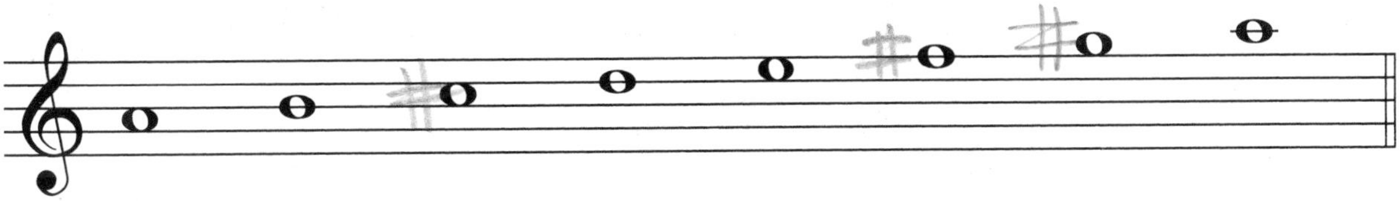

A Major Scale

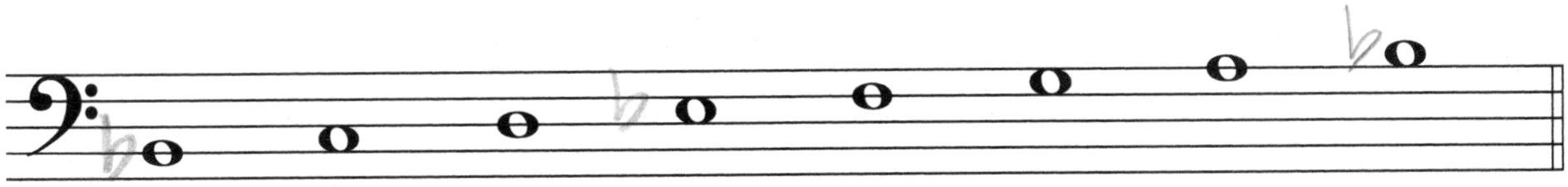

B♭ Major Scale

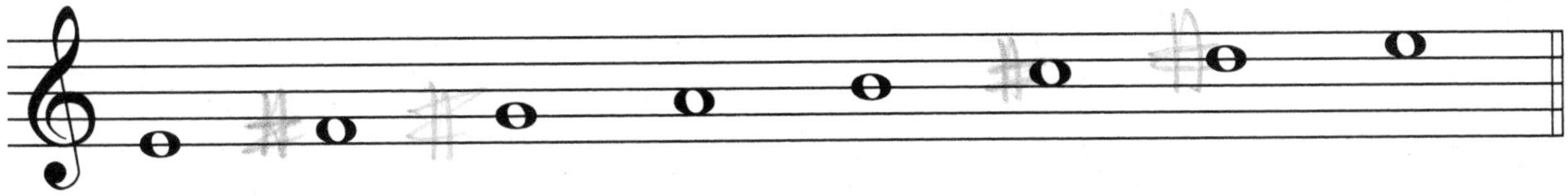

E Major Scale

F♯ Major Scale

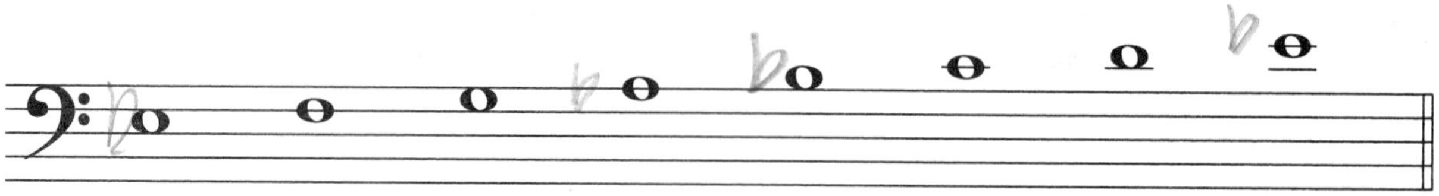

E♭ Major Scale

2. Draw these scales. Do not use key signatures. Draw sharps or flats before the notes.

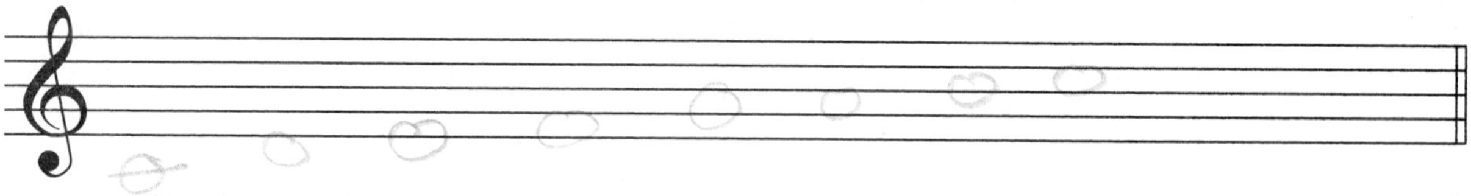

C Major Scale

B♭ Major Scale

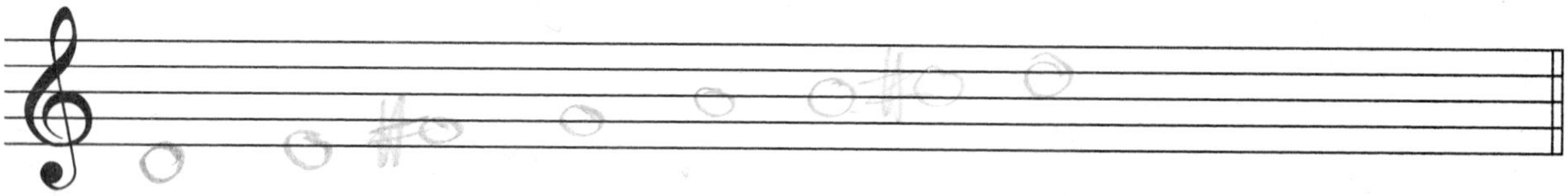

D Major Scale

A♭ Major Scale

G Major Scale

C♭ Major Scale

C♯ Major Scale

F Major Scale

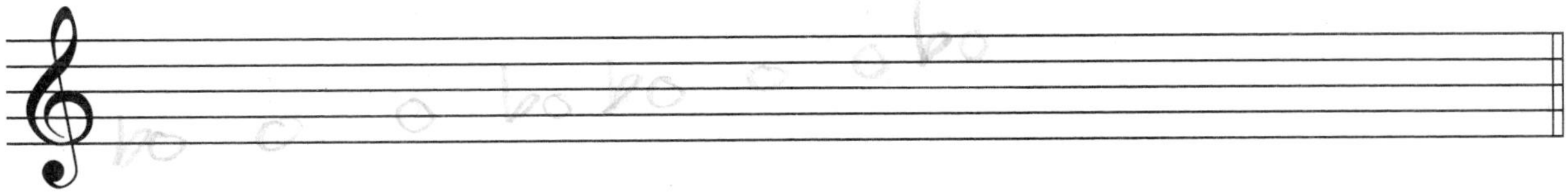

E♭ Major Scale

A Major Scale

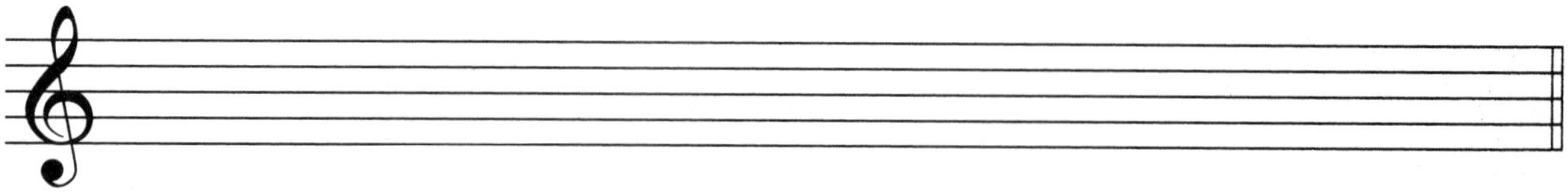

B Major Scale

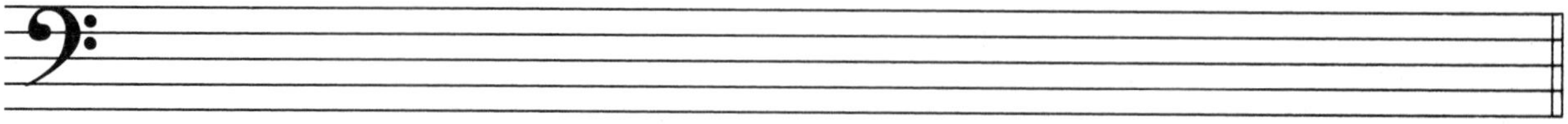

D♭ Major Scale

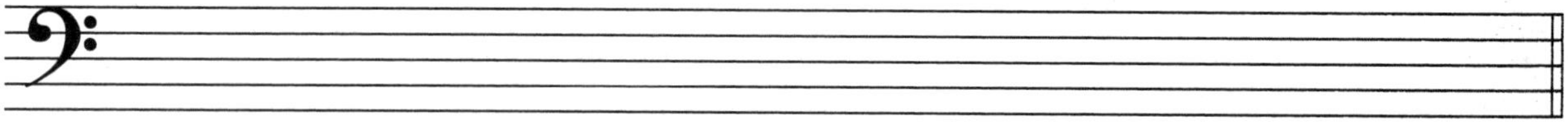

E Major Scale

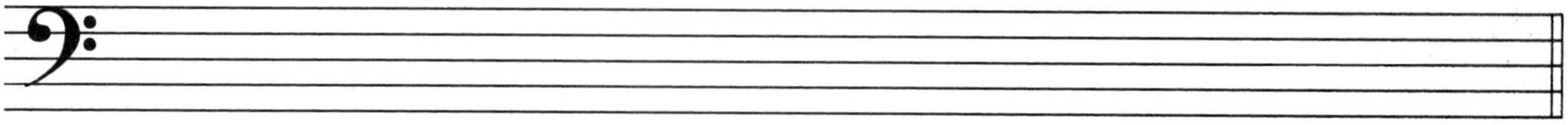

G♭ Major Scale

LESSON 3
MINOR KEY SIGNATURES AND SCALES

Most Major keys have a **RELATIVE MINOR.** The relative minor is found by going down three half steps from the name of the Major key.

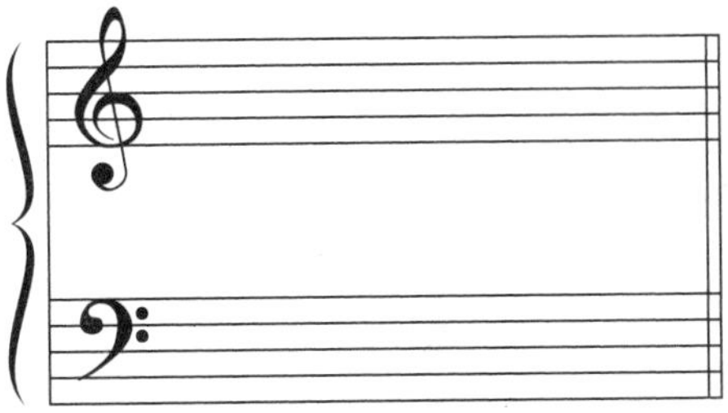

KEY SIGNATURE FOR C MAJOR

THREE HALF STEPS BELOW C IS A

KEY OF A MINOR

PARALLEL MAJOR and MINOR keys have the same letter name, such as C Major and c minor.

One way to determine whether a composition is in the Major key or in the minor key is to look at the last note of the music. It is usually the same as the name of the key. For example, if the music is in the key of e minor it will probably end on E. Also, look for the note around which the music is centered; which note appears to be the main note of the composition.

1. Write the name of the relative minor for each of the following Major keys. Determine the relative minor by going down three half steps from the name of the Major key. The first one is given.

a. G Major ___e minor___

b. E♭ Major ___c minor___

c. C Major ___a minor___

d. F Major ___d minor___

e. B♭ Major ___g minor___

f. D Major ___b minor___

2. Write the name of the relative Major for each of the following minor keys. Determine the relative Major by going <u>up</u> three half steps. The first one is given.

a. d minor F Major

b. e minor GM

c. c minor EbM

d. a minor CM

e. g minor BbM

f. b minor DM

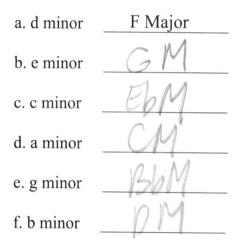

3. Name these minor keys. Determine the name of the Major key, then go down three half steps to find the relative minor. The first one is given.

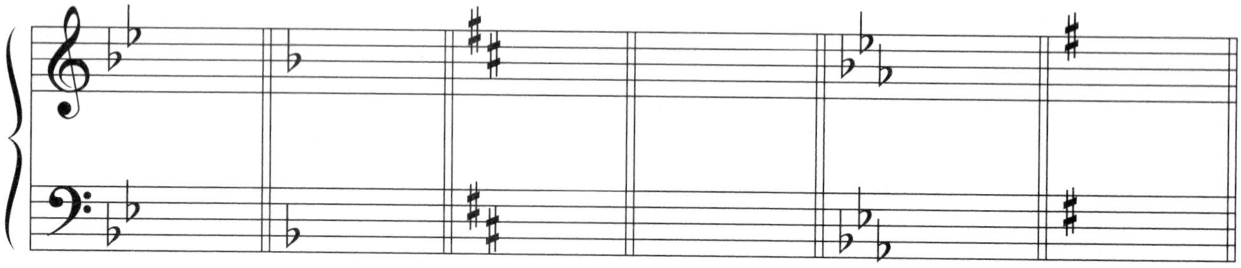

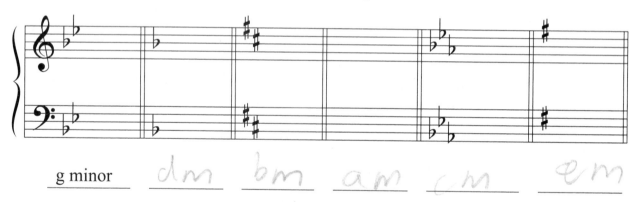

g minor dm bm am cm em

4. Draw the key signatures for these minor keys in both clefs. Go up three half steps to find the relative Major, then draw the key signature for that Major key. The first one is given.

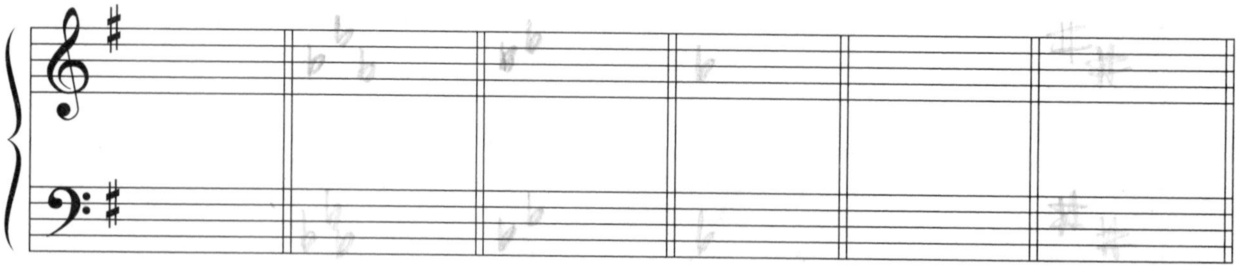

e minor c minor g minor d minor a minor b minor

5. Match these minor key signatures with their names by drawing lines to connect them.

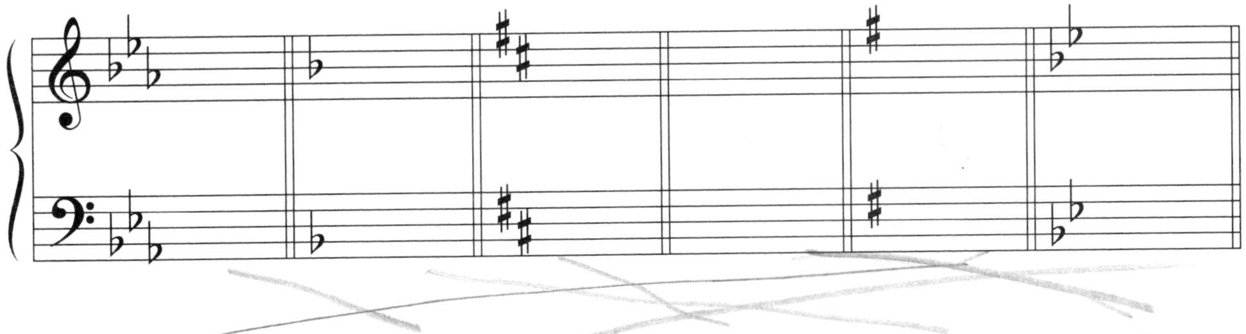

e minor c minor g minor b minor d minor a minor

6. Memorize these minor key signatures.

a minor	No sharps or flats	relative of C Major
e minor	F♯	relative of G Major
b minor	F♯ C♯	relative of D Major
d minor	B♭	relative of F Major
g minor	B♭ E♭	relative of B♭ Major
c minor	B♭ E♭ A♭	relative of E♭ Major

Like Major scales, **NATURAL MINOR SCALES** have eight notes that are separated by steps. They begin and end with notes of the same letter name, and include the sharps or flats that are in the minor key signature with the same name.

Example: d natural minor scale begins and ends with the note "D," and has B♭.

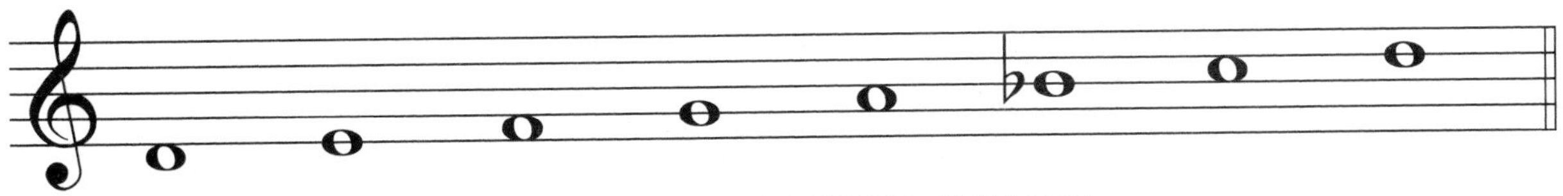

D NATURAL MINOR SCALE

7. Draw the sharps or flats from the minor key signature before the notes to complete each of these scales. The first one is given.

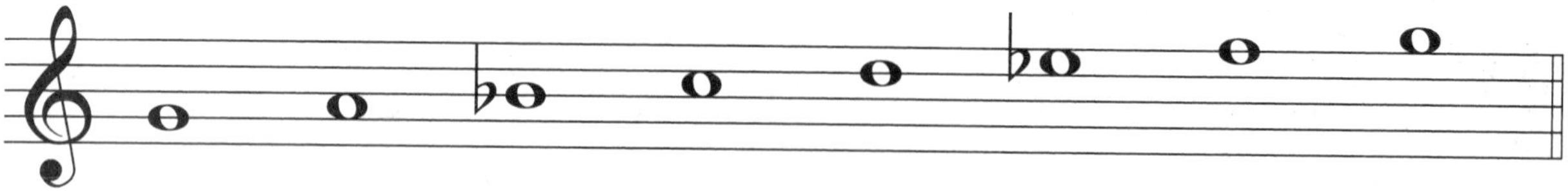

g natural minor scale

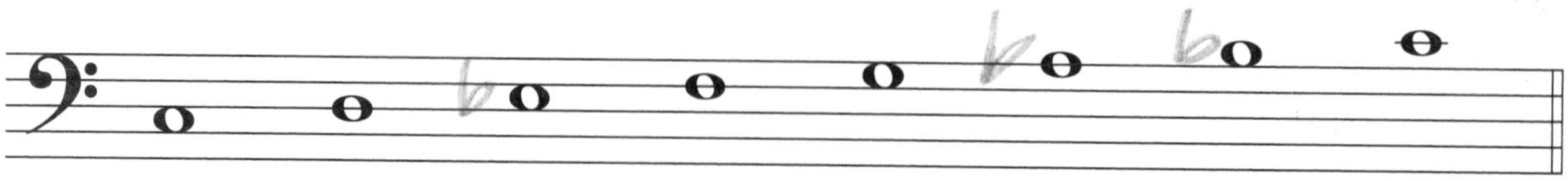

c natural minor scale

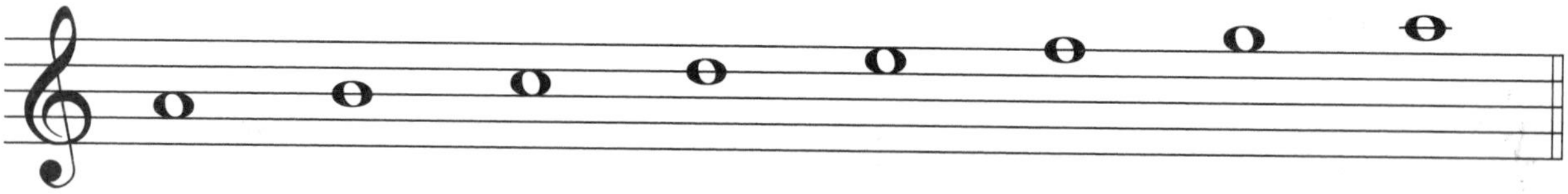

a natural minor scale

d natural minor scale

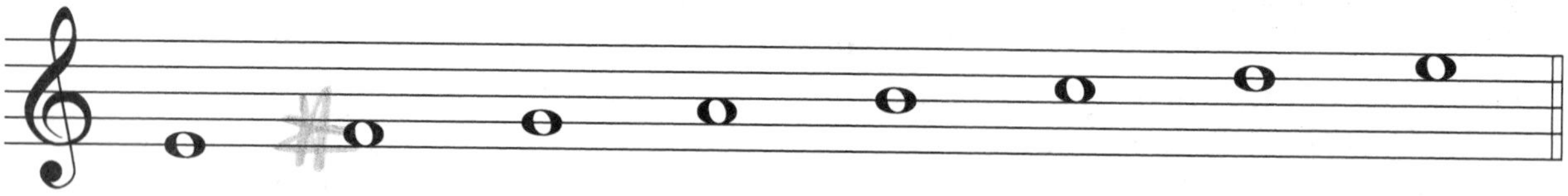

e natural minor scale

b natural minor scale

8. Draw these natural minor scales. Do not use key signatures. Draw sharps or flats before the notes. The first one is given.

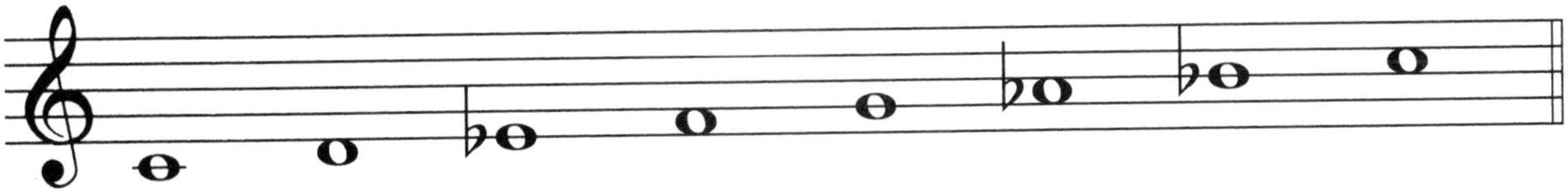

c natural minor scale

d natural minor scale

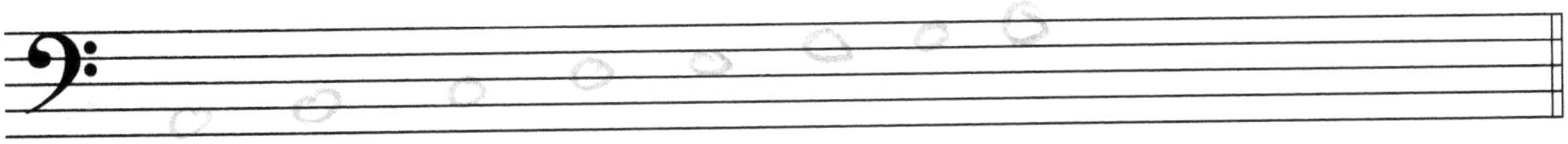

a natural minor scale

g natural minor scale

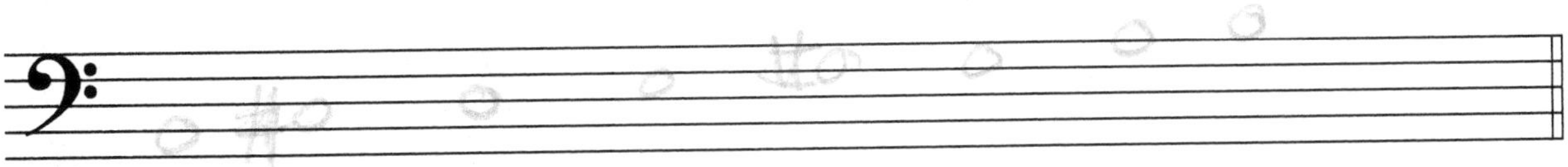

b natural minor scale

e natural minor scale

<u>HARMONIC MINOR SCALES</u> are created by raising the 7th note of the scale a half step. This creates a half step, rather than a whole step, between the 7th and 8th notes of the scale, making the 7th note a "leading tone."

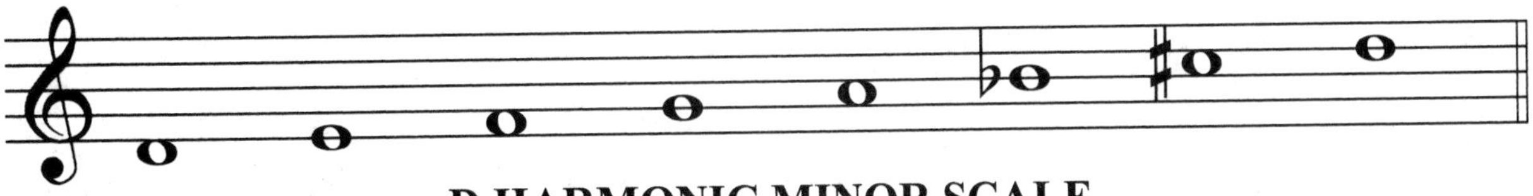

D HARMONIC MINOR SCALE

9. Draw these harmonic minor scales. Do not use key signatures. Draw sharps or flats before the notes.

c harmonic minor scale

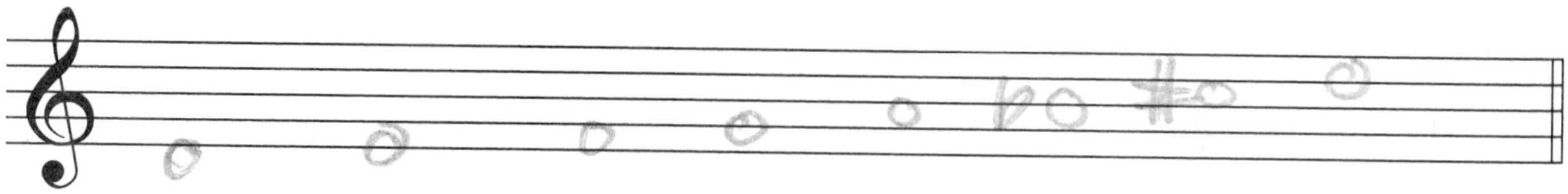

d harmonic minor scale

a harmonic minor scale

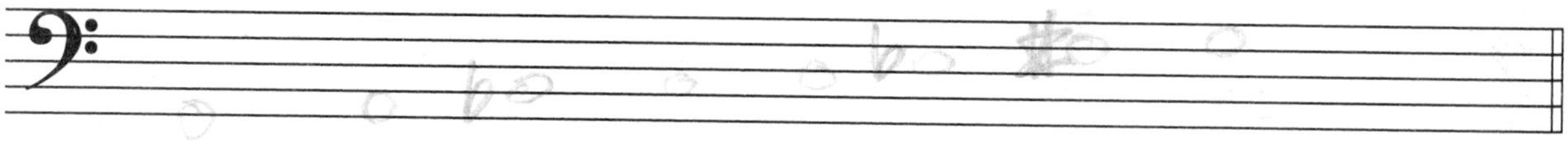

g harmonic minor scale

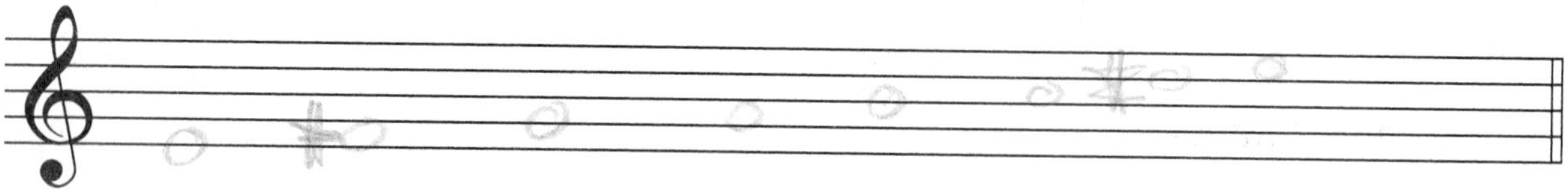

e harmonic minor scale

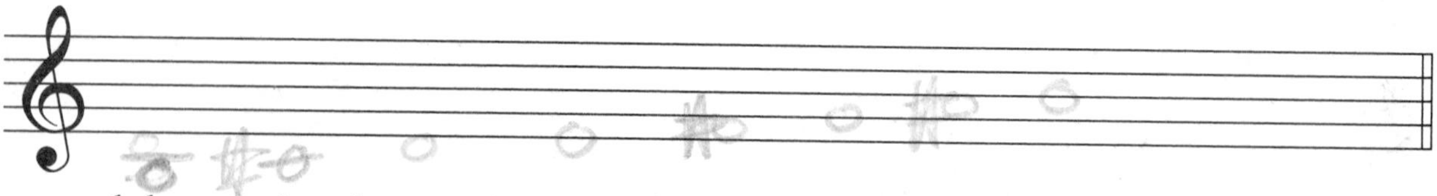

b harmonic minor scale

LESSON 4
INTERVALS

An **INTERVAL** is the distance between two notes. Intervals are named with qualities and numbers.

When naming intervals, count the two notes that form the interval and all the lines and spaces (or all the letter names) between the two notes.

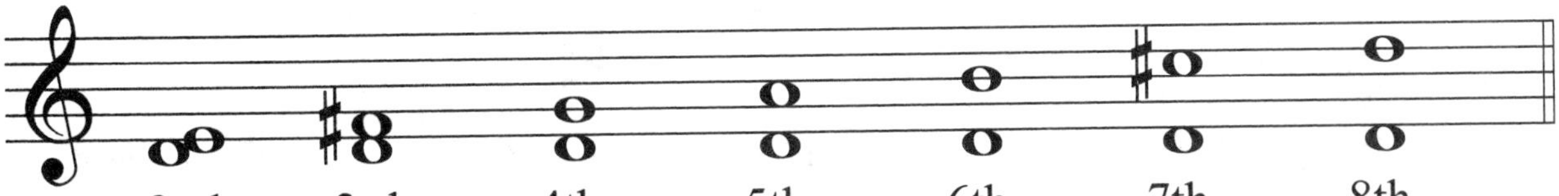

2nd 3rd 4th 5th 6th 7th 8th

If the top note of the interval is within the key of the bottom note, the interval is **Major** or **Perfect**. **2nds, 3rds, 6ths,** and **7ths** are **Major**. **4ths, 5ths,** and **8ths** (octaves) are **Perfect**.

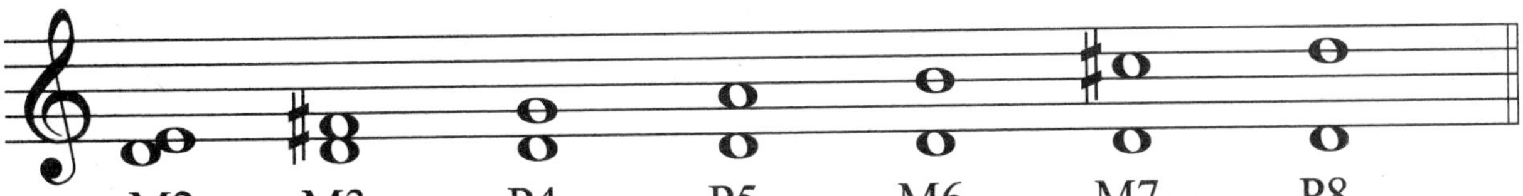

M2 M3 P4 P5 M6 M7 P8 (Octave)

1. Name these intervals with their qualities (Major or Perfect) and numbers (2nd, 3rd, etc.). The first one is given.

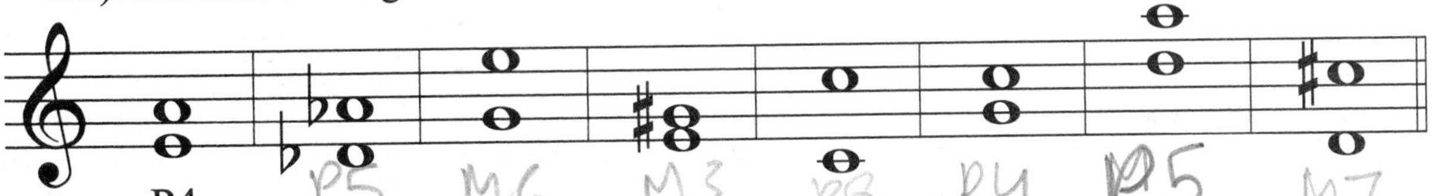

P4 __P5__ __M6__ __M3__ __P8__ __P4__ __P5__ __M7__

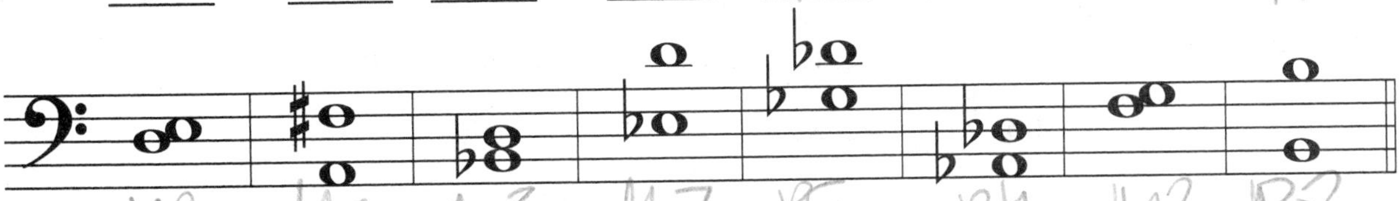

__M2__ __M6__ __M3__ __M7__ __P5__ __P4__ __M2__ __P8__

2. Draw a note above each given note to complete these intervals. Include any sharps or flats that are in the key signature of the given note. The first one is done for you.

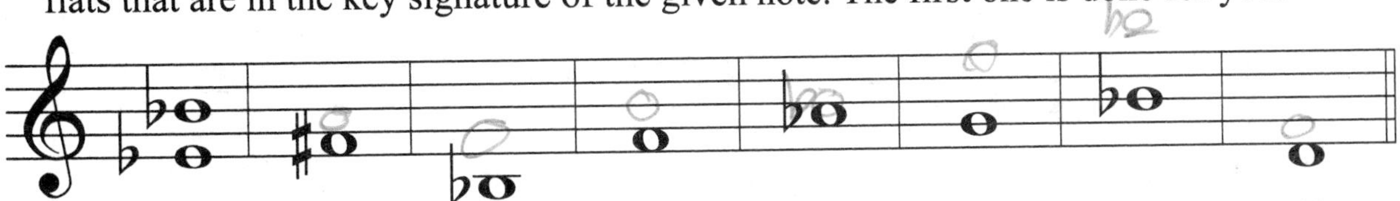

P5 M3 M6 P4 M2 M7 P8 (Octave) M3

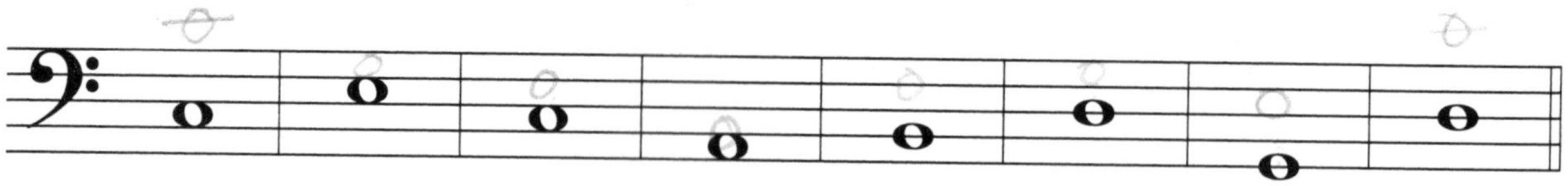

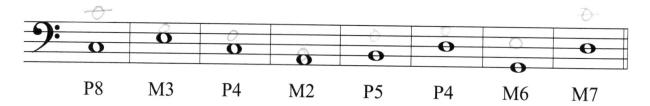

P8 M3 P4 M2 P5 P4 M6 M7

If the top note of a **Major 2nd, 3rd, 6th,** or **7th** is lowered a half-step without changing the letter name of the note, the interval becomes **minor**.

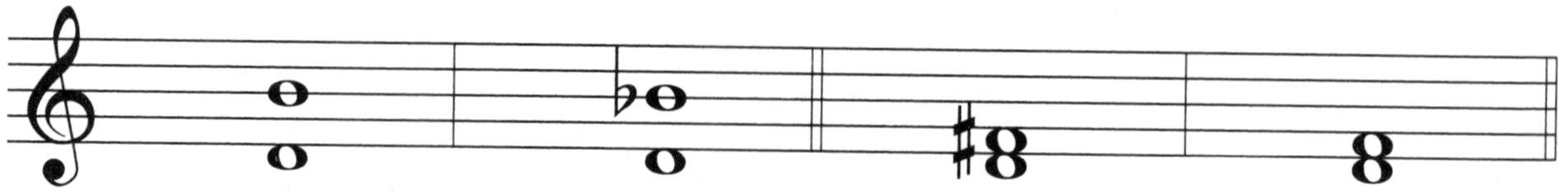

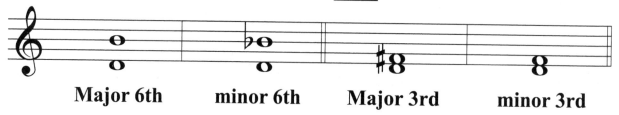

Major 6th **minor 6th** **Major 3rd** **minor 3rd**

3. Name these intervals with their qualities (Major, Perfect, or minor), and numbers (2nd, 3rd, etc.). The first one is given.

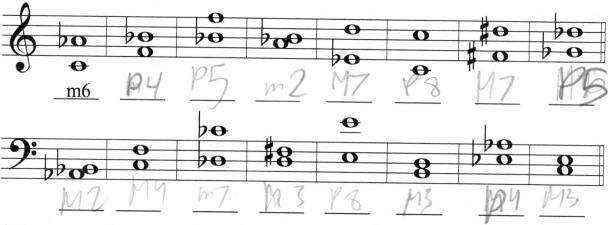

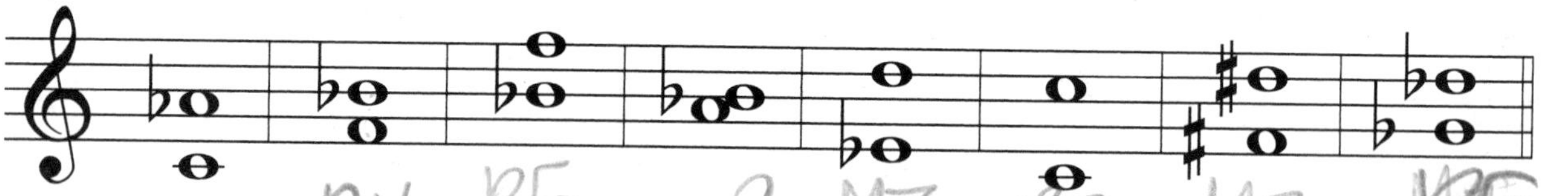

m6

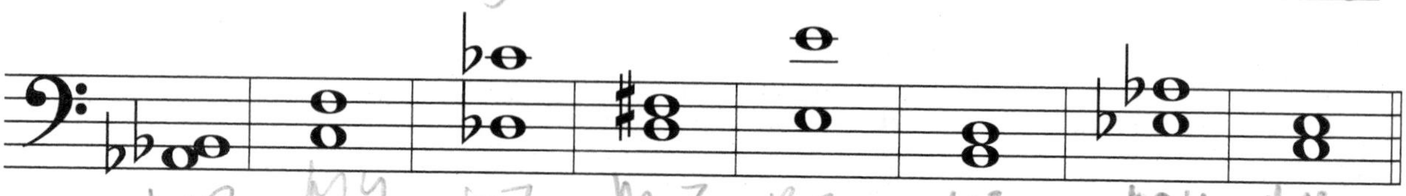

4. Draw a note above each given note to complete these intervals.

- For Major and Perfect intervals, include any sharps or flats from the key signature of the given note.
- For minor intervals, determine the note that forms a Major interval, then lower the note a half-step.

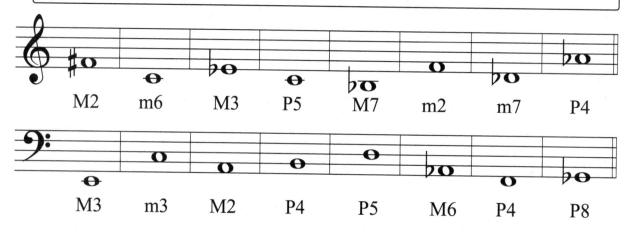

M2 m6 M3 P5 M7 m2 m7 P4

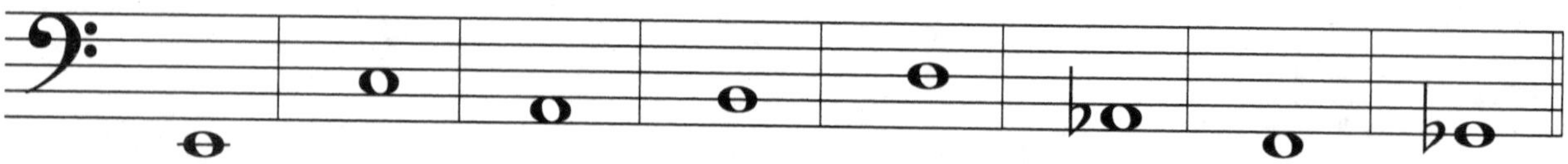

M3 m3 M2 P4 P5 M6 P4 P8

Two ways to form an interval below a note:

1. Find the letter name by counting down through the lines and spaces.
2. Determine the quality of the interval that you just created.
3. If needed, adjust the lower note to create the correct quality.

Example: M3 below G

1. Three notes below G is E.

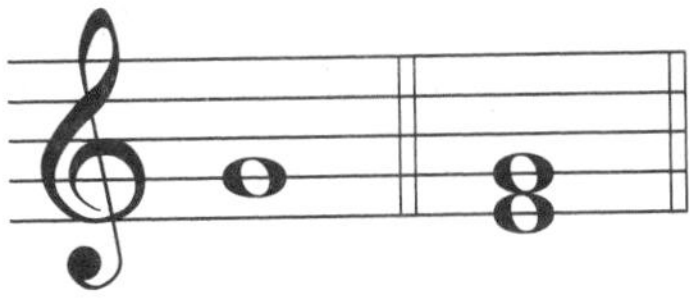

2. The resulting interval is a minor 3rd.

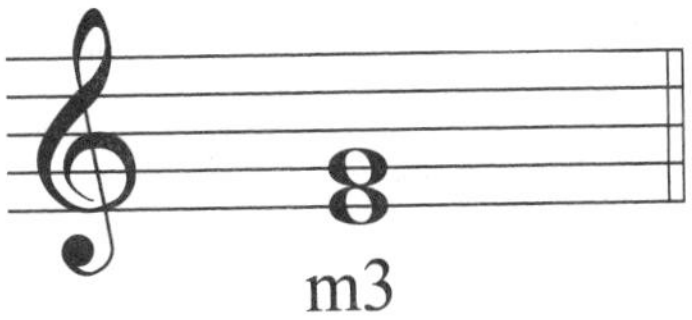

m3

3. Change the E to E♭ to make the interval Major.

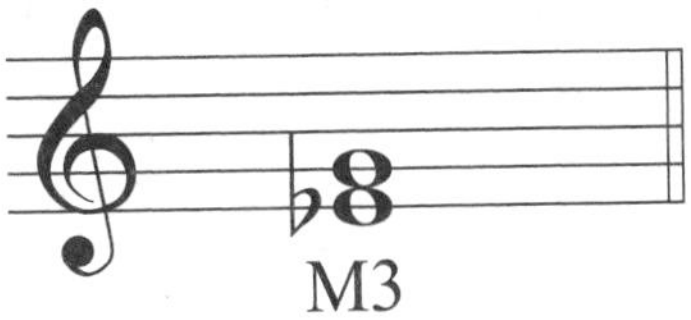

M3

---

1. Determine all possibilities the note could be.
2. Determine which of those notes is the correct one for the quality of the interval.

Example: Major 7th below C

1. The three possibilities are D, D♭, and D♯.
2. The key of D♭ Major has C, D Major has C♯, and a M7 above D♯ would be C double sharp.
3. The answer is D♭.

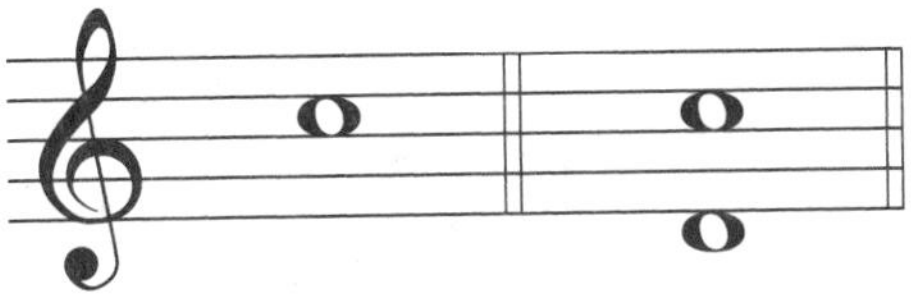

M7 down | D♭ Major has C

5. Draw a note <u>below</u> each given note to complete these intervals. The first one is given.

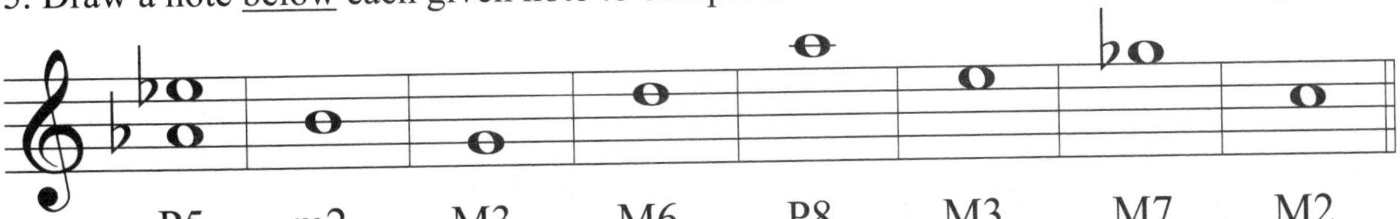

P5 m2 M3 M6 P8 M3 M7 M2

m3 P4 M2 m7 m2 m6 m3 P4

To name an interval in a composition:

a. Draw the sharps or flats from the key signature or from earlier in the measure before the notes.

b. Determine the number.

c. Using the key signature of the **low note of the interval**, determine the quality (Major, Perfect, or minor).

a. Draw flat - B♭

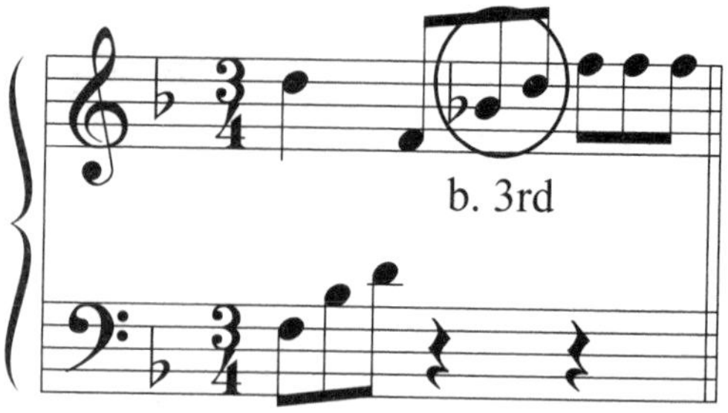

c. Use **B♭ Major** key signature; B♭ to D is a Major 3rd

6. Name the circled intervals in each of the following phrases.

a. From *Allegro Scherzando* by Haydn.

b. From *Elfin Dance* by Grieg.

c. From *Polonaise* by Mozart.

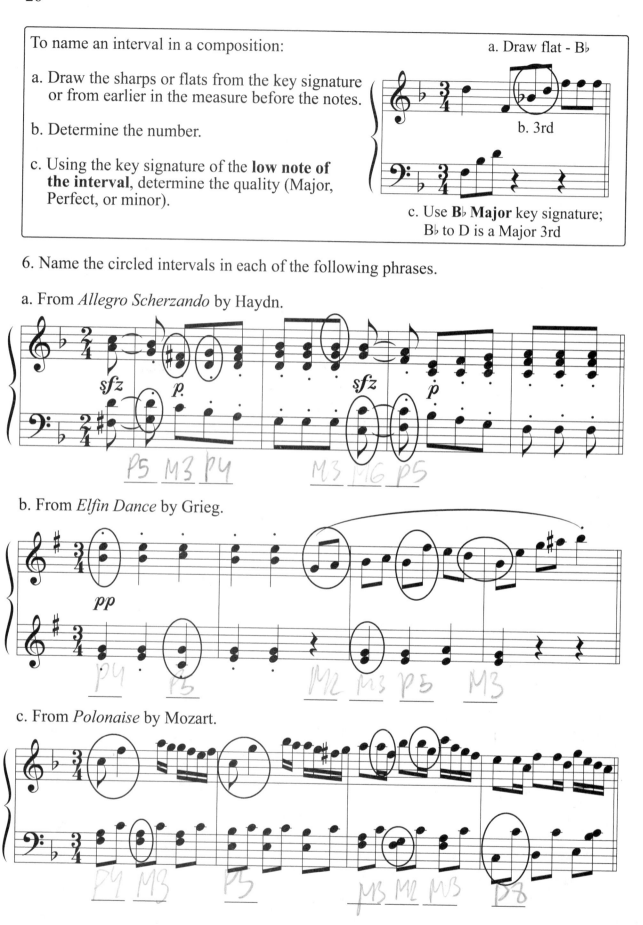

LESSON 5
MAJOR, MINOR, AND DIMINISHED TRIADS

A **TRIAD** is a three note chord, based on the interval of a third. Triads are named with letter names and qualities.

D MAJOR TRIAD

MAJOR TRIADS are made up of the first, third, and fifth notes of the Major scale that has the same letter name. The notes are called **ROOT**, **THIRD**, and **FIFTH**.

When the triad is in its simplest position (with the notes each a third apart), the lowest note of the triad is the **ROOT.** The root gives the triad its letter name.

There is a Major 3rd between the root and the third, and a minor third between the third and the fifth.

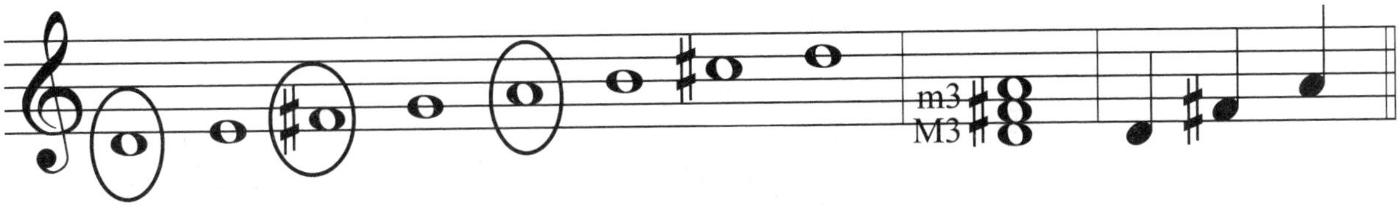

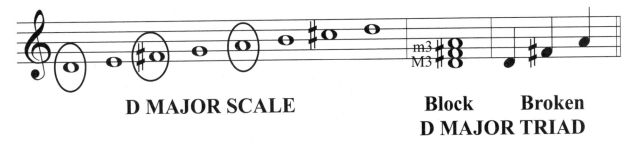

D MAJOR SCALE **Block** **Broken**
D MAJOR TRIAD

1. Draw each of the following triads. The first one is given.

> • Each triad should only have line notes or space notes.
> • Add any sharps or flats from the key signature of the root.

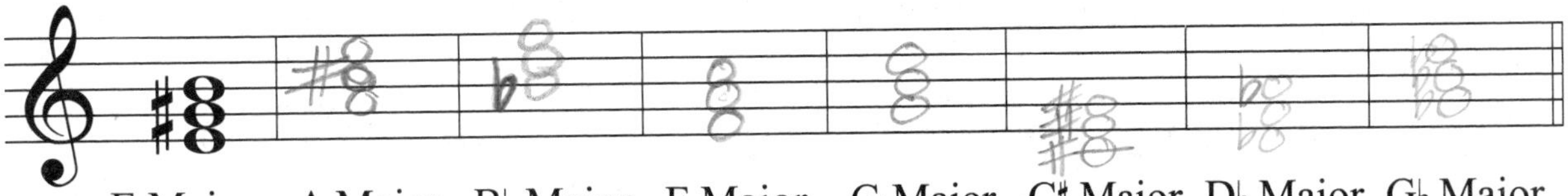

E Major A Major B♭ Major F Major G Major C♯ Major D♭ Major G♭ Major

F♯ Major E♭ Major B Major D Major C Major A♭ Major C♭ Major E Major

To change a Major triad into a **MINOR** triad, lower the third a half-step.

Minor triads have the same sharps or flats as the minor key signature with the same name.

There is a minor 3rd between the root and the third, and a Major 3rd between the third and the fifth.

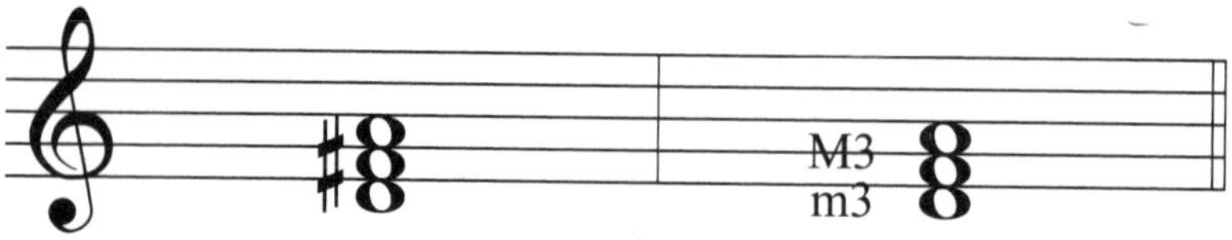

D Major Triad **d minor triad**

2. Draw each of the following triads. To lower a flat a half-step, use a double flat: 𝄫.

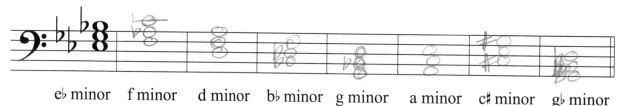

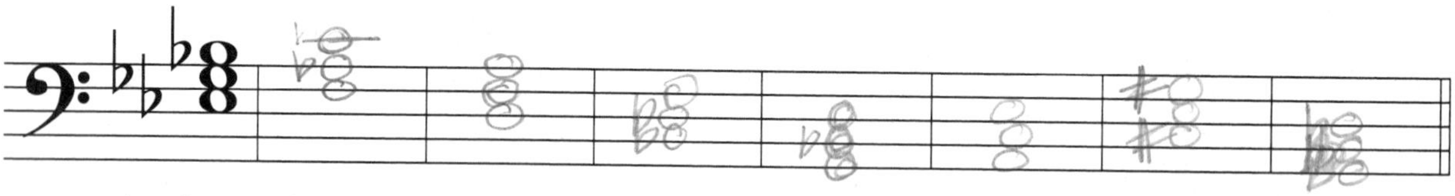

e♭ minor f minor d minor b♭ minor g minor a minor c♯ minor g♭ minor

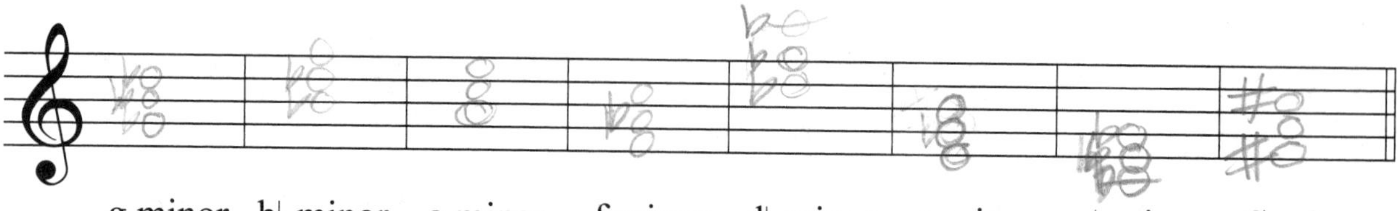

g minor b♭ minor a minor f minor d♭ minor e minor c♭ minor f♯ minor

To change a Major triad into a **DIMINISHED** triad, lower the third and the the fifth a half-step.

The intervals between the root and the third and between the third and the fifth are minor thirds.

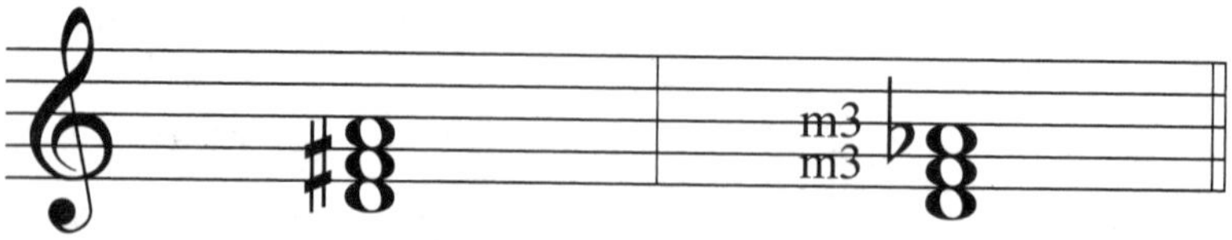

D Major Triad **d diminished triad**

3. Draw each of the following triads. The first one is given.

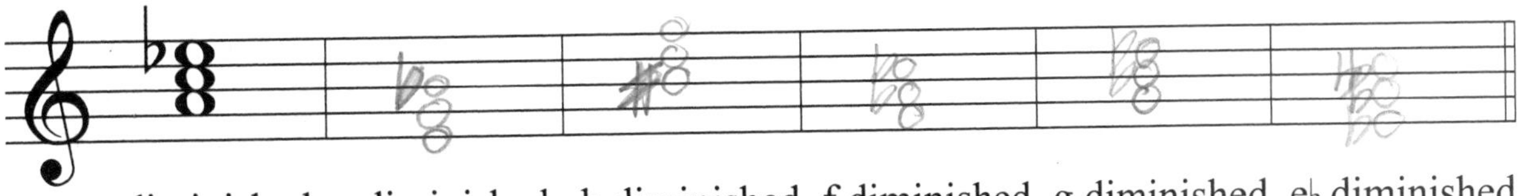

a diminished e diminished b diminished f diminished g diminished e♭ diminished

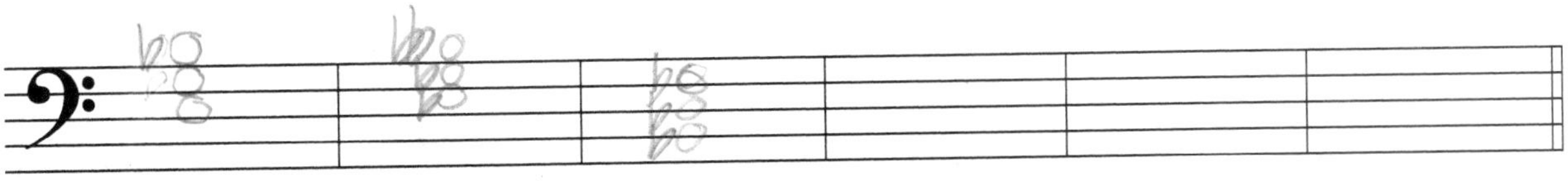

e diminished e♭ diminished b♭ diminished d diminished c diminished a♭ diminished

4. Name each of the following triads with its root (letter name) and quality (Major, minor, or diminished). The first one is given.

f minor e major c minor ab major eb major bb minor cb major d# minor

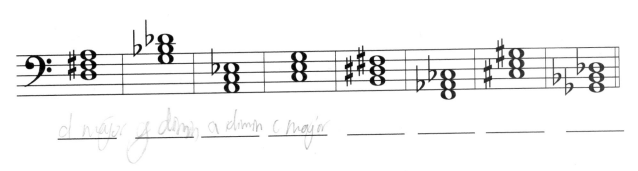

d major g dimin a dimin c major ______ ______ ______ ______

5. Draw each of the following triads.

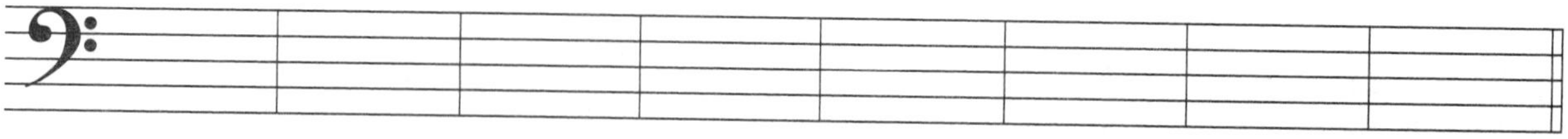

D Major g minor B♭ Major f diminished c minor A Major D♭ Major c♭ minor

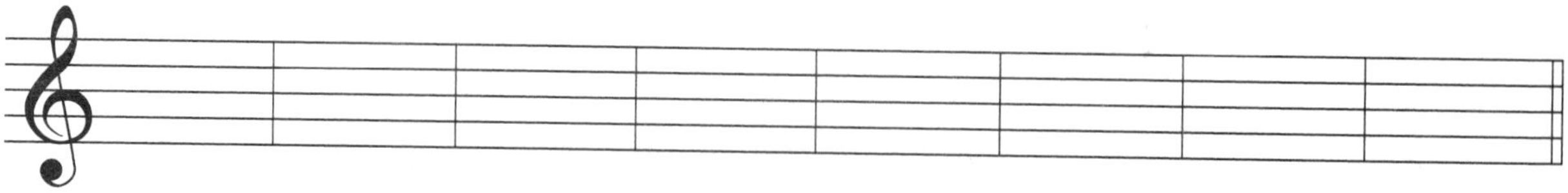

d minor E Major e♭ minor g diminished A♭ Major e minor C♯ Major g♭ minor

TRIAD CHART

CHORD	MAJOR	MINOR	DIMINISHED
C F G	No ♯ or ♭	♭ 3rd	♭ 3rd and 5th
D A E	♯ 3rd	No ♯ or ♭	♭ 5th
D♭ A♭ E♭	♭ root and 5th	♭ all notes	♭ root and 3rd, ♭♭ 5th
C♭ G♭	♭ all notes	♭ root and 5th, ♭♭ 3rd	♭ root, ♭♭ 3rd and 5th
F♯ C♯	♯ all notes	♯ root and 5th	♯ root
B♭	♭ root	♭ root and 3rd	♭ all notes
B	♯ 3rd and 5th	♯ 5th	No ♯ or ♭

LESSON 6
INVERSIONS OF TRIADS

A **ROOT POSITION TRIAD** occurs when the **root** of the triad is lowest. **FIGURED BASS** is used to identify the position. The figured bass symbol for root position is $^{5}_{3}$, because when the triad is in its simplest position, the intervals above the lowest note are a 5th and a 3rd. When labeling a triad in root position, figured bass is optional.

Sometimes the letter R is used instead of figured bass.

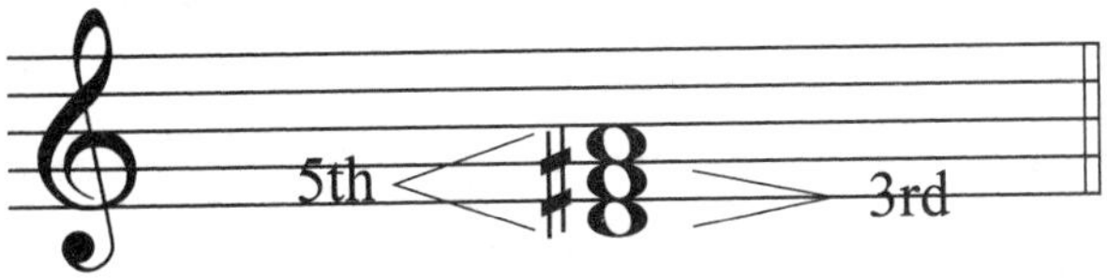

D Major Root Position Triad

D Major

D Major $^{5}_{3}$

D Major R

A **FIRST INVERSION TRIAD** occurs when the **third** of the triad is lowest. The figured bass symbol for first inversion is $^{6}_{3}$, because when the triad is in its simplest position, the intervals above the lowest note are a 6th and a 3rd. In this simple position, **the top note of the triad is the root.**

When labeling first inversion triads, the figured bass symbol ^{6} or $^{6}_{3}$ is written to the right of the name of the triad.

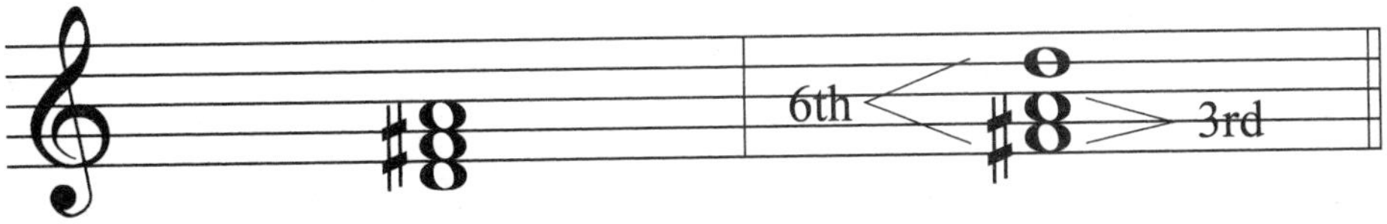

D Major
Root Position Triad

D Major
First Inversion Triad

D Major ^{6}

D Major $^{6}_{3}$

D Major 1st

A **SECOND INVERSION TRIAD** occurs when the **fifth** of the triad is lowest. The figured bass symbol for second inversion is $^6_4$, because when the triad is in its simplest position, the intervals above the lowest note are a 6th and a 4th. In this simple position, **the middle note of the triad is the root.**

When labeling second inversion triads, the figured bass symbol $^6_4$ is used.

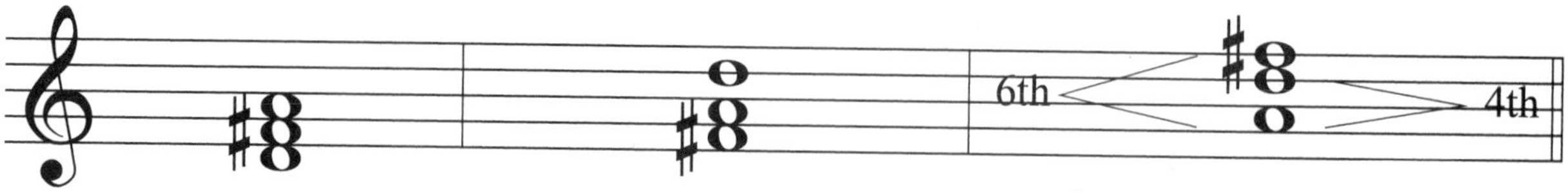

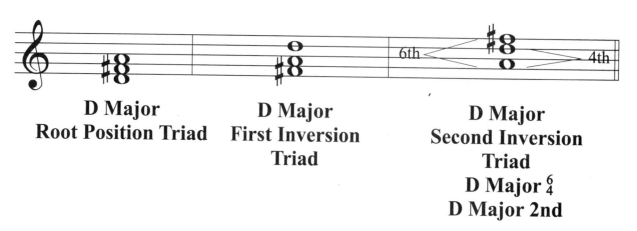

D Major Root Position Triad	D Major First Inversion Triad	D Major Second Inversion Triad D Major $^6_4$ D Major 2nd

1. Name these triads with their roots (letter names), qualities, and inversions. The first one is given.

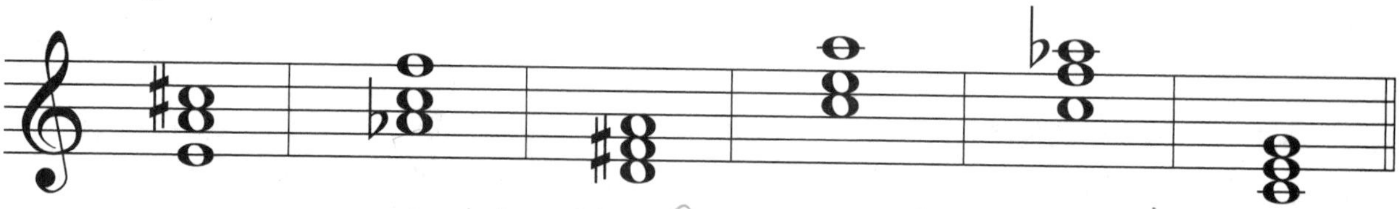

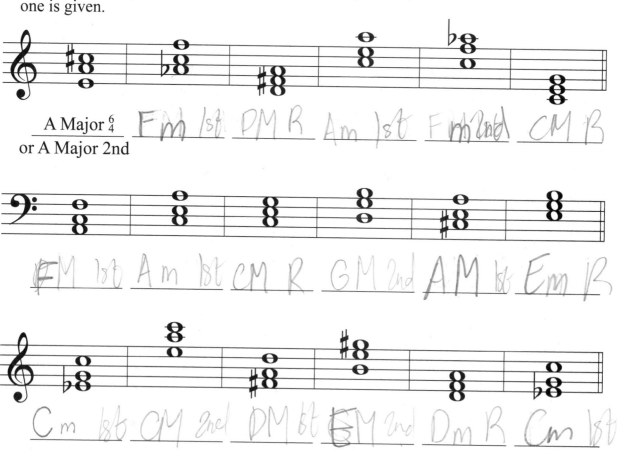

A Major $^6_4$ or A Major 2nd | Fm 1st | DM R | Am 1st | Fm 2nd | CM R

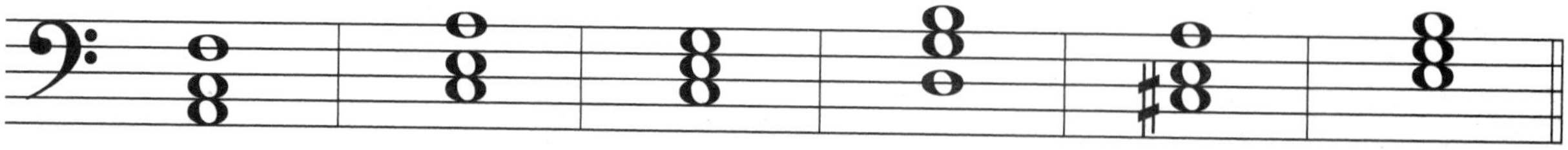

FM 1st | Am 1st | CM R | GM 2nd | AM 1st | Em R

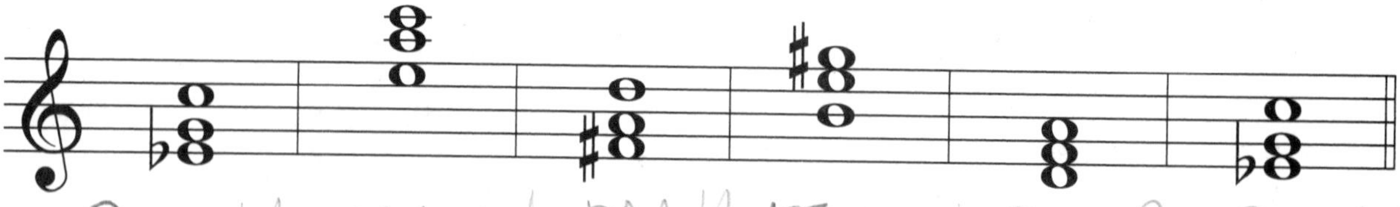

Cm 1st | CM 2nd | DM 1st | EM 2nd | Dm R | Cm 1st

2. Draw each of the following triads. Fill in each root. The first one is given.

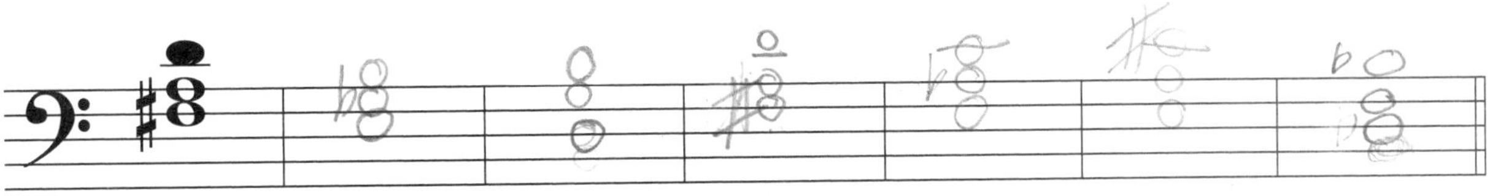

D Major ^{6} e minor G Major $^6_4$ d minor $^6_3$ f minor $^5_3$ A Major $^6_4$ B♭ Major ^{6}

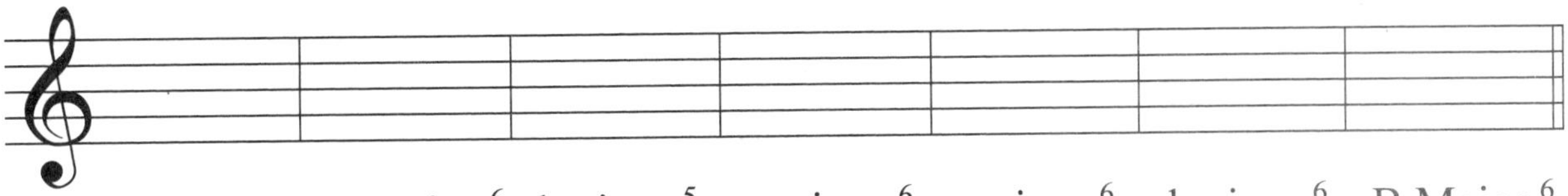

E Major F Major ^{6} d minor $^5_3$ e minor $^6_4$ c minor $^6_3$ d minor $^6_4$ B Major $^6_4$

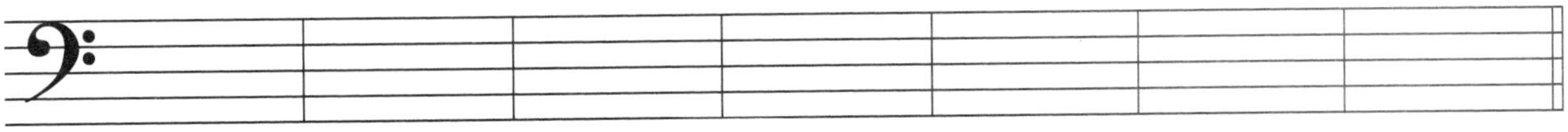

C Major $^6_4$ A Major $^6_3$ g minor $^5_3$ a minor ^{6} E Major $^6_3$ F Major $^6_4$ e♭ minor ^{6}

3. Draw these triads in root position, first inversion, and second inversion. The first one is given.

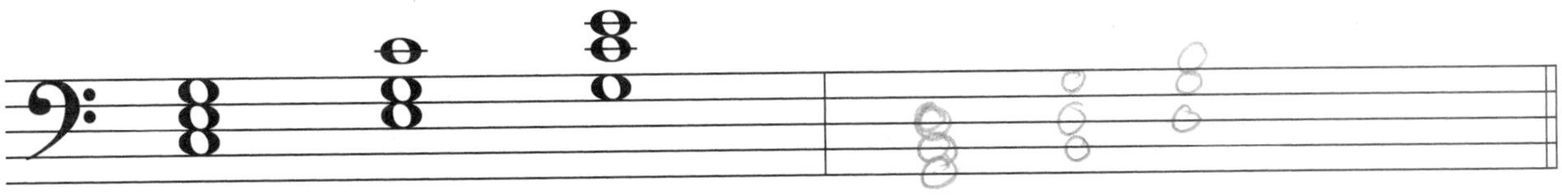

C Major G Major

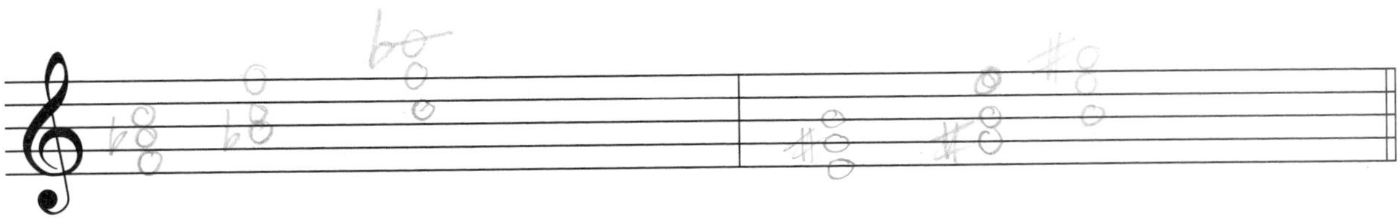

f minor E Major

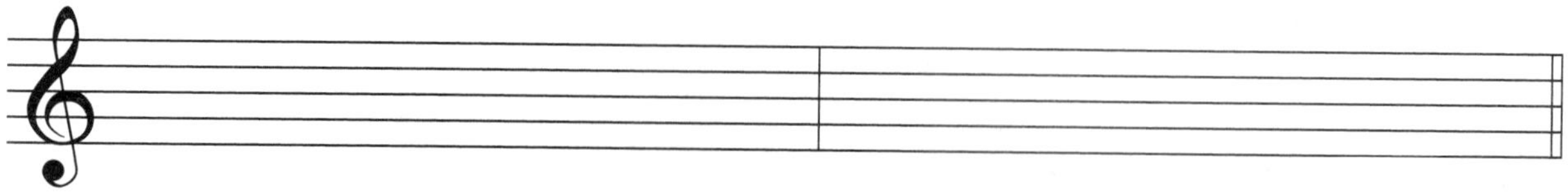

e minor

d minor

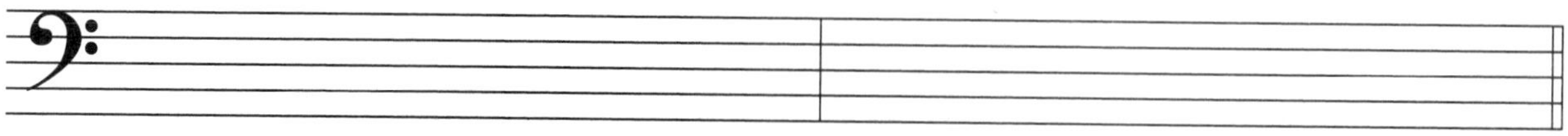

a minor

F Major

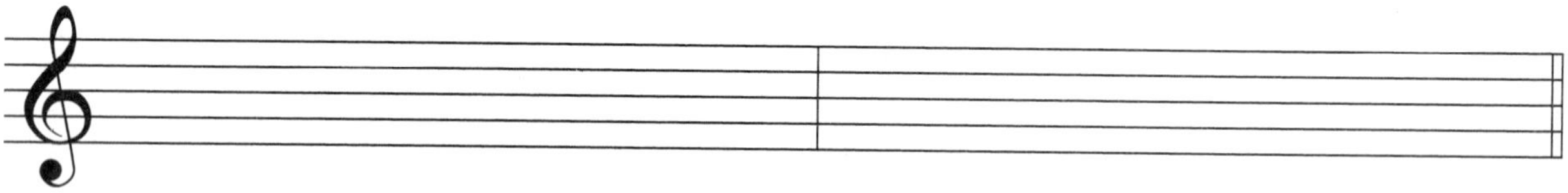

g minor

c minor

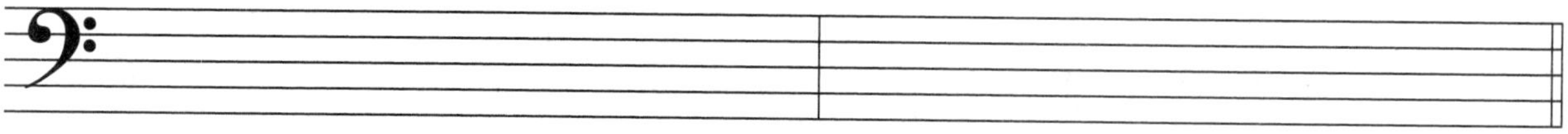

D Major

A Major

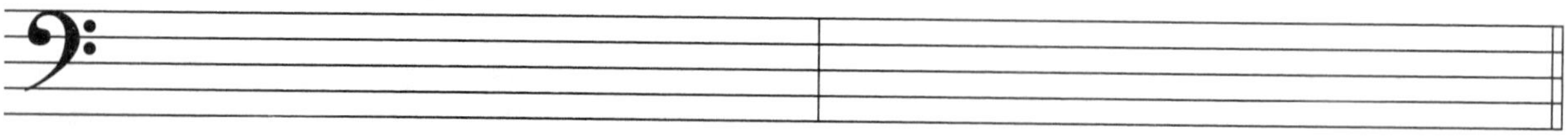

b♭ minor

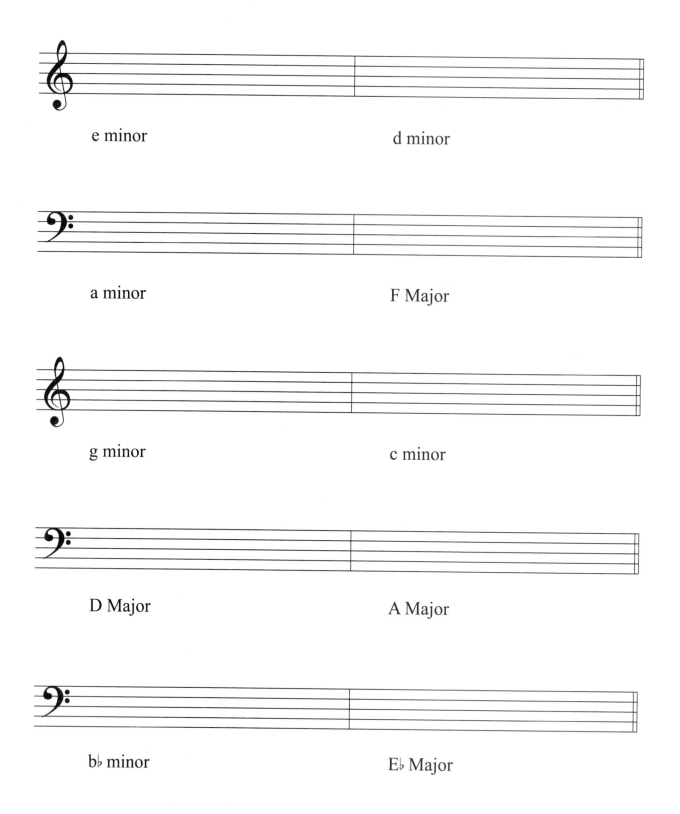

E♭ Major

LESSON 7
TRIADS AND INVERSIONS IN MUSIC LITERATURE

In actual music, triads are rarely in their simplest positions. To determine the root, quality, and inversion of a triad within a composition, follow these steps:

a. Put the triad in its simplest form by placing the letter names so that there is one letter between each (for example, F-C-F-A becomes F-A-C), or draw the root position triad on a staff.

b. Add any sharps or flats from the key signature or from earlier in the measure to the notes.

c. Name the triad with its root and quality.

d. Determine the inversion of the triad by looking at the lowest note on the <u>lowest</u> staff.

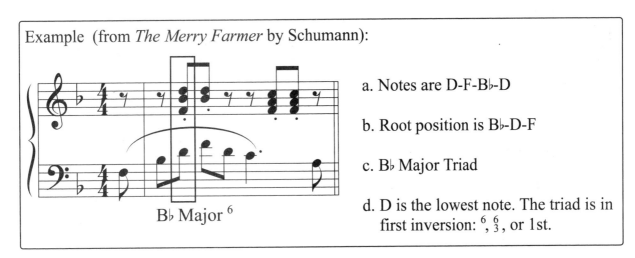

Example (from *The Merry Farmer* by Schumann):

B♭ Major ^{6}

a. Notes are D-F-B♭-D

b. Root position is B♭-D-F

c. B♭ Major Triad

d. D is the lowest note. The triad is in first inversion: ^{6}, $^6_3$, or 1st.

1. Name each boxed triad with its root, quality, and inversion. The first one is given.

a. From *Ballade* by Burgmüller.

c minor $^6_4$ (c minor 2nd) | C minor 1st | G Major 2nd | C minor root

Eb G C | D G B → G B D | C G Eb / C Eb G

b. From *Allegro Scherzando* by Haydn.

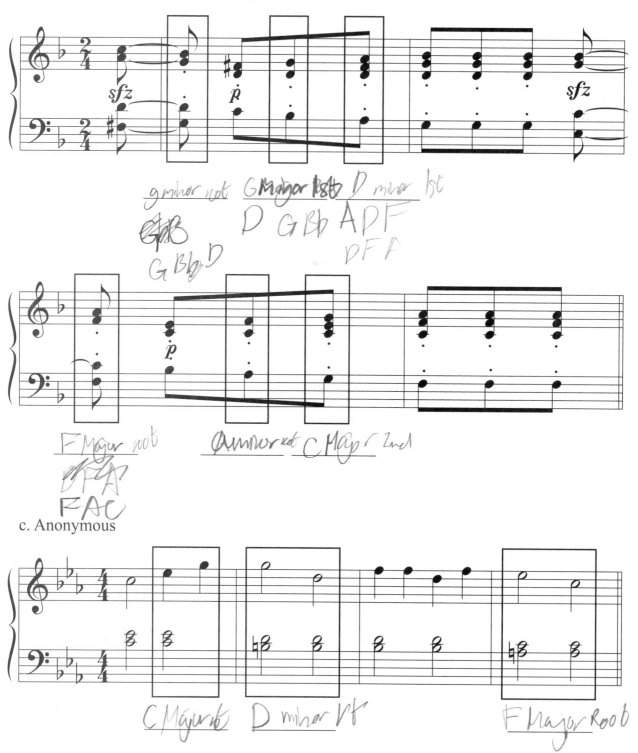

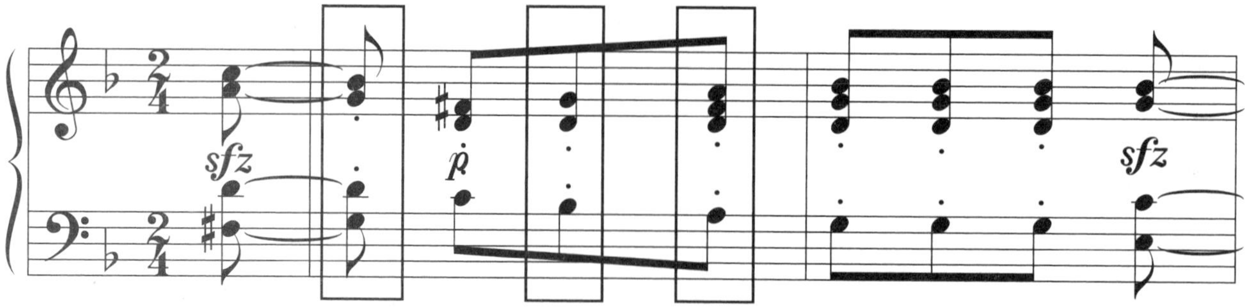

g minor root G Major 1st D minor 1st

D G Bb A D F

G Bb D D F A

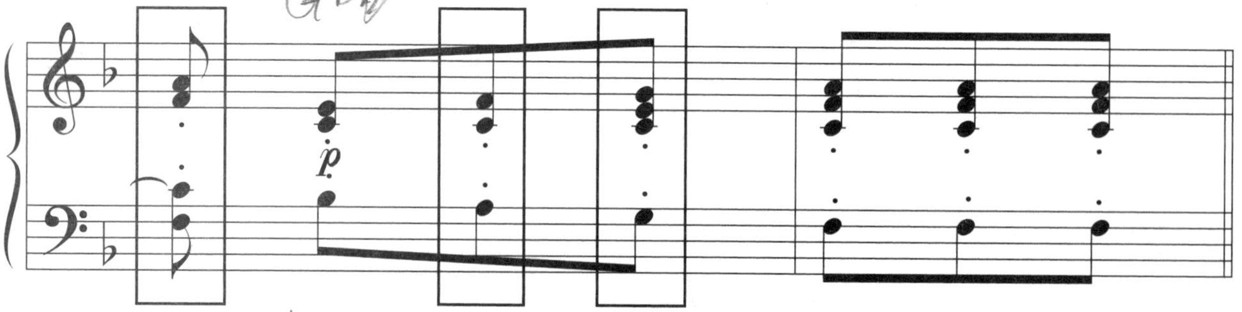

F Major root D minor root C Major 2nd

FAC

c. Anonymous

C Major root D minor F Major Root

LESSON 8
PRIMARY AND SECONDARY TRIADS

A triad can be built on each note of the scale.

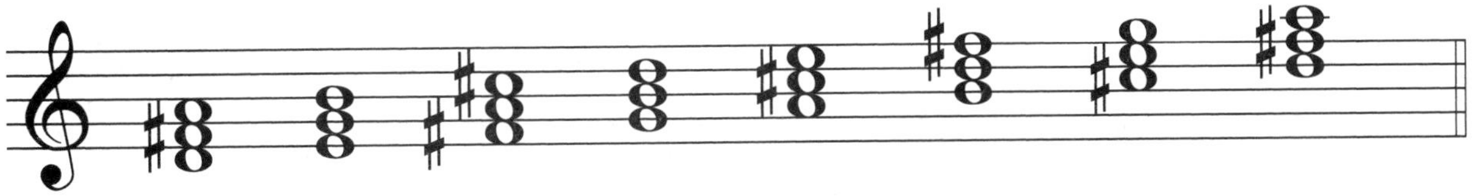

Triads Built on the Notes of D Major Scale

When building triads on scale tones, all of the sharps or flats that are in the scale (or key signature) must be added to the chords which have those notes.

Example: D Major Scale has F♯ and C♯. When drawing the triads of D Major, every time an F or C appears in a chord, a sharp must be added to it, as shown in the example above.

Triads of the scale are numbered using Roman numerals. Upper case Roman numerals are used for Major triads, lower case Roman numerals are used for minor triads, upper case Roman numerals with $^{+}$ are used for Augmented triads,* and lower case Roman numerals with ° are used for diminished triads.

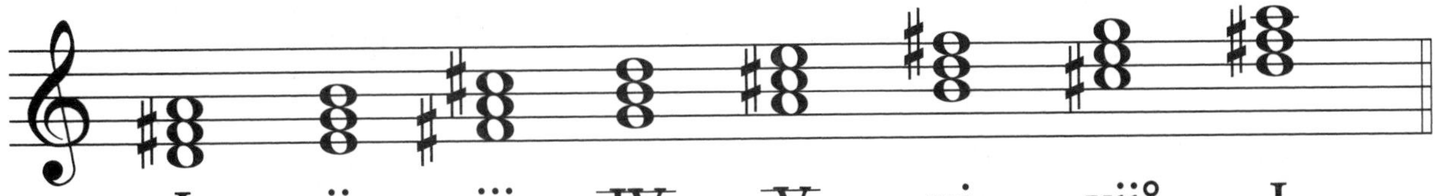

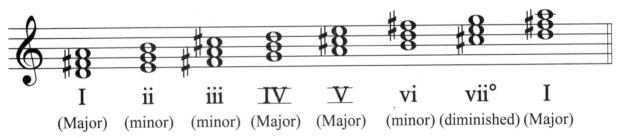

I	ii	iii	IV	V	vi	vii°	I
(Major)	(minor)	(minor)	(Major)	(Major)	(minor)	(diminished)	(Major)

<u>**I, IV, and V**</u> are the <u>**PRIMARY TRIADS**</u>. In Major keys, these three triads are Major. They are the most common chords for harmonizing tonal melodies. The chords are labeled with upper case Roman numerals.

<u>**ii, iii, vi, and vii°**</u> are the <u>**SECONDARY TRIADS**</u>. In Major keys, ii, iii, and vi are minor, and vii° is diminished. The chords are labeled with lower case Roman numerals, and the vii° chord has a small circle beside the Roman numeral.

> When Roman numerals are hand-written, lines are typically drawn above and below the Roman numerals for Major chords. When Roman numerals are computer-generated, the distinction between capital and lower-case letters is obvious, so the lines are not needed.

*Augmented triads are created by raising the top note of a Major triad a half step

The qualities of the triads in minor keys are different from those for Major keys. When using harmonic minor, the triads have the following qualities:

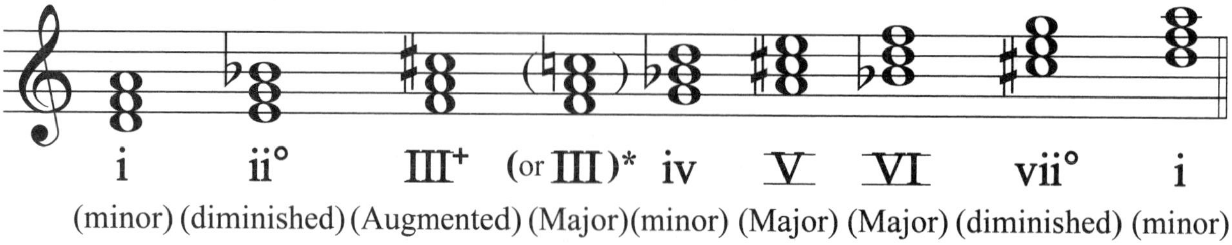

Primary and Secondary Triads in the Key of d minor

i is minor.
ii° is diminished.
III+ may be Augmented or Major
iv is minor.
V is Major.
VI is Major.
vii° is diminished.

1. Draw the primary and secondary triads for these keys, and label the triads with Roman numerals. Draw lines above and below the Roman numerals for Major chords. Circle each primary triad and put a box around each secondary triad. Do not use key signatures. Draw sharps or flats before the notes. The first one is given.

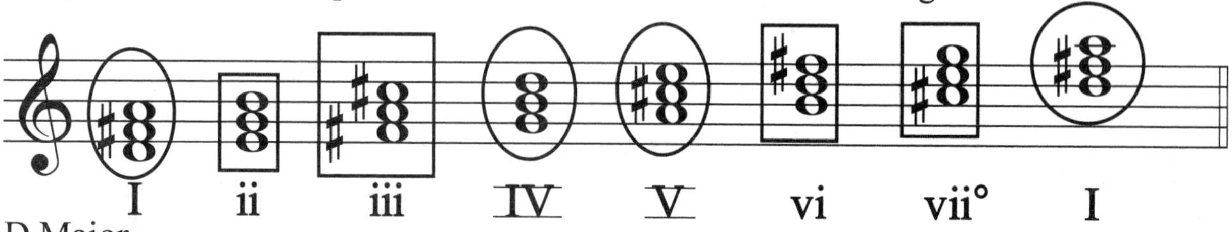

D Major

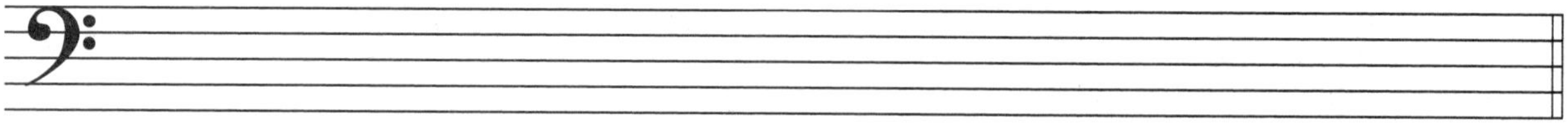

G Major

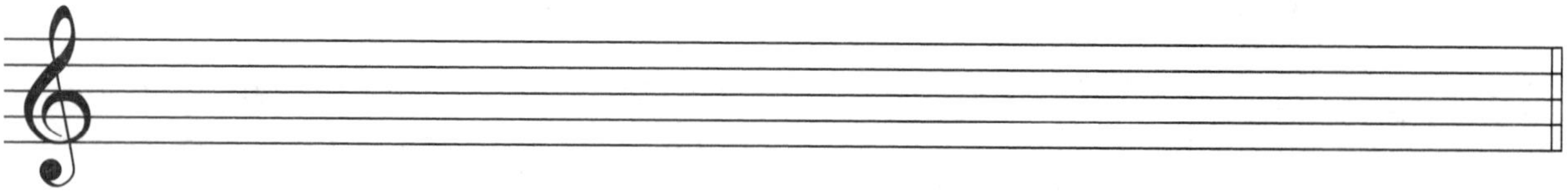

F Major

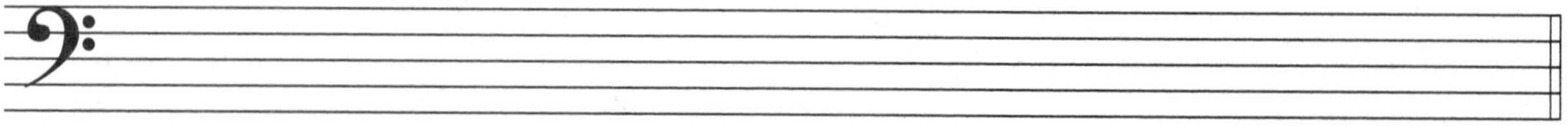

a harmonic minor

*In music, the III chord in minor keys is usually Major. III+ is rare.

2. Draw the primary triads for these keys, and label them with Roman numerals. Draw lines above and below the Roman numerals. Do not use key signatures. Draw sharps or flats before the notes. The first one is given.

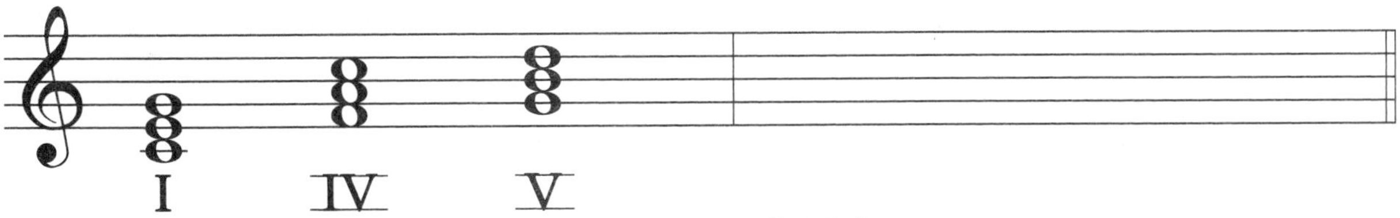

C Major

G Major

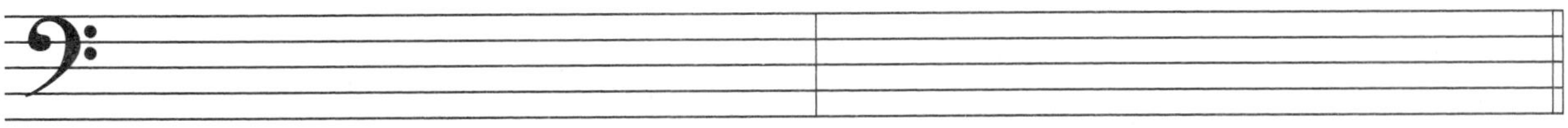

a harmonic minor

F Major

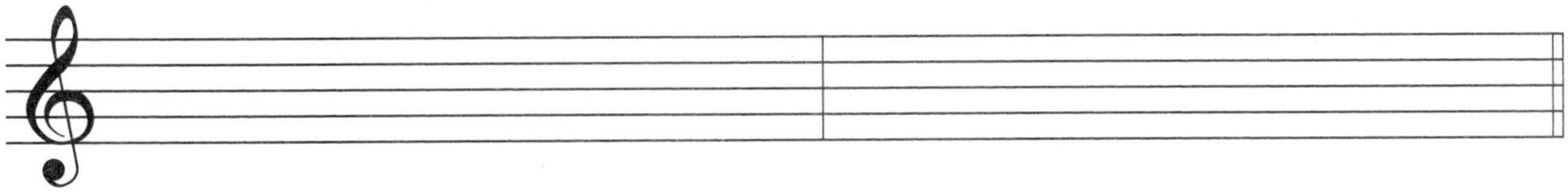

E Major

D Major

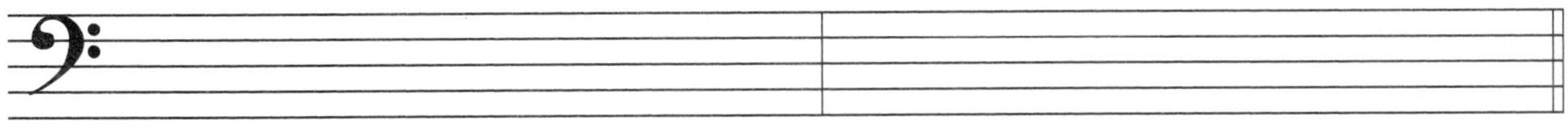

A Major

C Major

3. Draw the secondary triads for these keys, and label the chords with Roman numerals. Do not use key signatures. Draw sharps or flats before the notes. The first one is given.

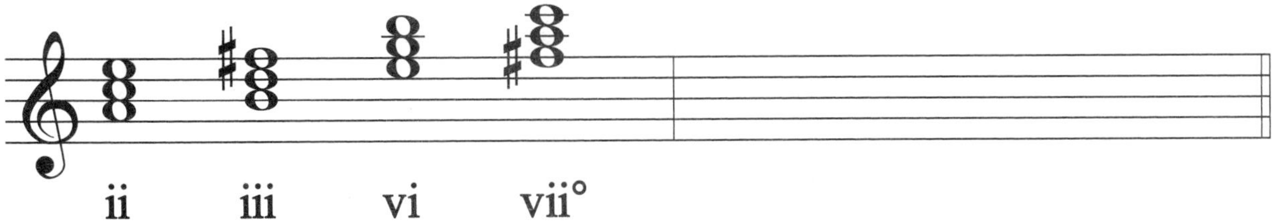

G Major

C Major

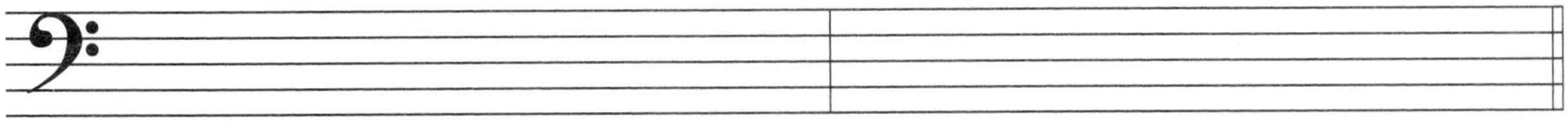

F Major

G Major

Each degree of the scale has a name. These are called the **SCALE DEGREE NAMES**.

The **I** chord is **TONIC**.

The **ii** chord is **SUPERTONIC**.

The **iii** chord is **MEDIANT**.

The **IV** chord is **SUBDOMINANT**.

The **V** chord is **DOMINANT**.

The **vi** chord is **SUBMEDIANT**.

The **vii°** chord is **LEADING TONE**.

4. Match these Roman numerals with their scale degree names.

a. ii	_____	Submediant
b. I	_____	Dominant
c. iii	_____	Supertonic
d. vii°	_____	Subdominant
e. IV	_____	Leading Tone
f. vi	_____	Mediant
g. V	_____	Tonic

5. Write the scale degree names for these Roman numerals.

I ______________________________

ii ______________________________

iii ______________________________

IV ______________________________

V ______________________________

vi ______________________________

vii° ______________________________

LESSON 9
ROMAN NUMERAL CHORD NAMES WITHIN A COMPOSITION

To determine the Roman numeral of a chord within a composition:

a. Determine the Major or minor key of the music.

b. Name the chord with its root and quality.

c. Determine the Roman numeral by counting from the name of the key up to the name of the chord.

d. Look at the lowest note on the lowest staff to determine the inversion.

Example (From *The Merry Farmer* by Schumann):

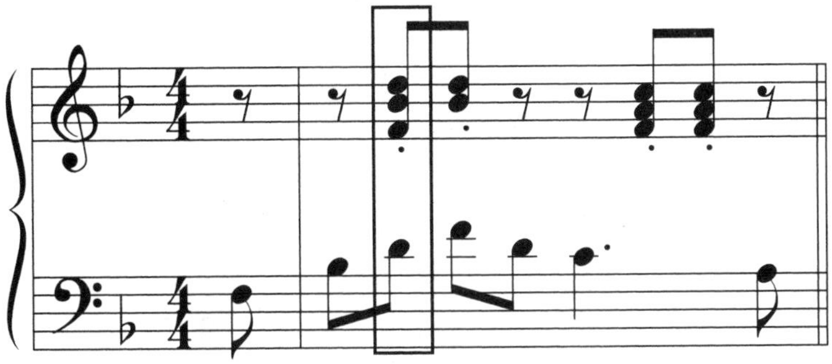

IV^{6}

IV^{6}_{3}

IV **R**

a. Key of F Major.

b. The chord is B♭ Major.

c. Count up from F to B♭. This is the IV chord.

e. The lowest note in the bass clef is D.The chord is in first inversion. Label the chord IV^{6}_{3}, IV^{6}, or IV 1st.

Tips:

1. Be sure to determine whether the music is in the Major key or the minor key.

2. Use upper-case Roman numerals for Major chords and draw lines above and below the Roman numerals.

3. Use lower-case Roman numerals for minor and diminished chords.

4. If the Roman numerals are unusual, such as a minor V chord, you may be using the wrong key. Double-check your key signature.

1. Name of the key for each of the following phrases. Label the boxed chords with Roman numerals and inversions. Draw lines above and below the Roman numerals for Major chords. The first one is given.

a. From *Arabesque* by Burgmüller. Key of: __a__ __minor______

b. From *Norse Song* by Schumann. Key of: _____ ______________

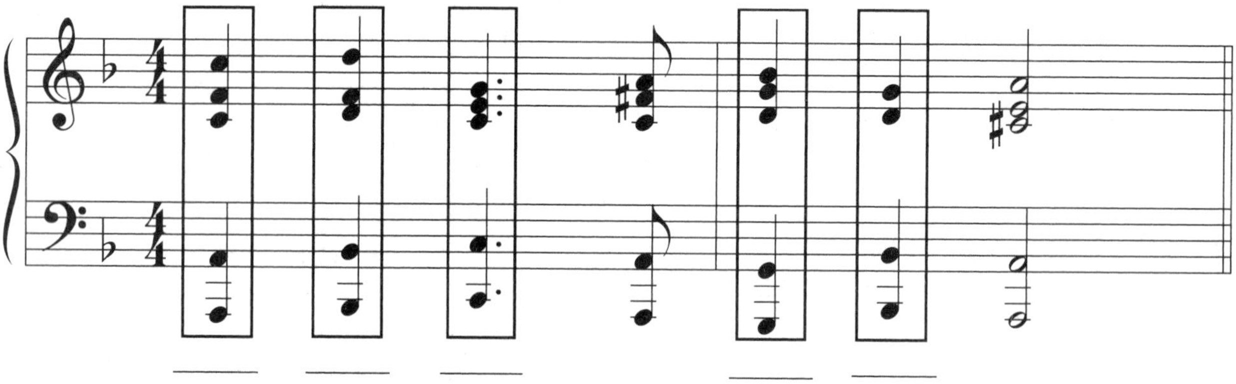

c. From *Humming Song* by Schumann. Key of: _____ ______________

d. Anonymous. Key of: _____ ______________

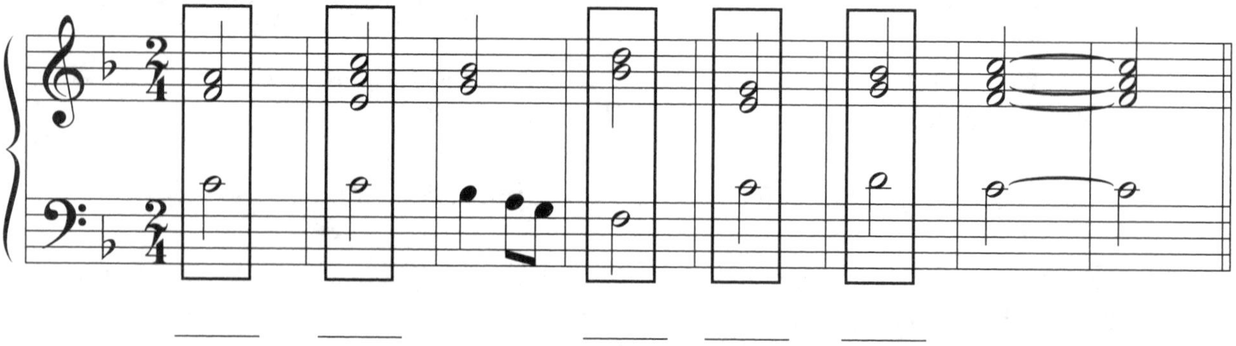

LESSON 10
THE DOMINANT SEVENTH CHORD

The **<u>DOMINANT SEVENTH CHORD</u>** is created by adding a note to a Major triad that is a minor seventh above the root. The Dominant Seventh chord has four different notes. The notes are called **ROOT, THIRD, FIFTH,** and **SEVENTH.** The chord is named Dominant 7th because typically it is built on the V or Dominant chord, and has the interval of a 7th within the chord.

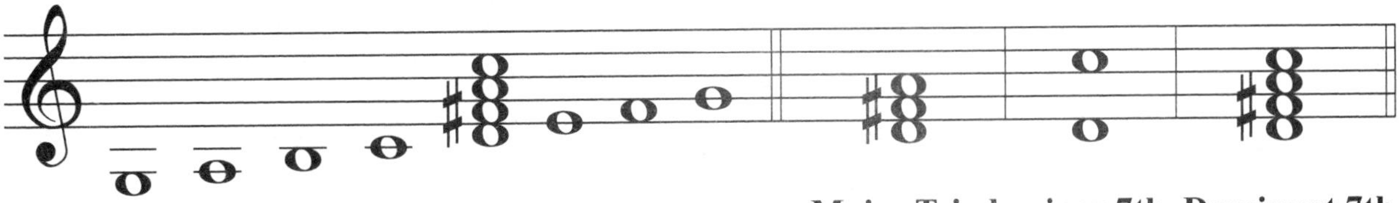

Dominant 7th in G Major (V 7) **Major Triad** **minor 7th** **Dominant 7th**

To draw a Dominant Seventh on a given root, draw a Major triad. Add a fourth note that is a minor seventh above the root.

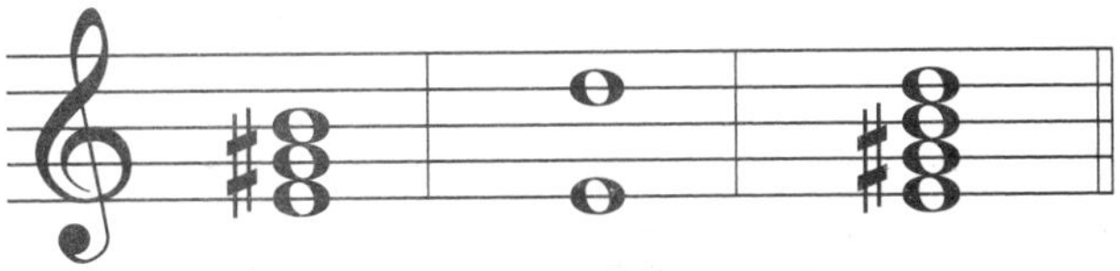

E Major Triad **m7 above E** **E Dominant 7th**

To draw a Dominant Seventh in a given key, draw the V chord for that key. Add a fourth note that is a minor 7th above the root. In Major keys, only the sharps or flats that are in the key signature will are added to the chord.

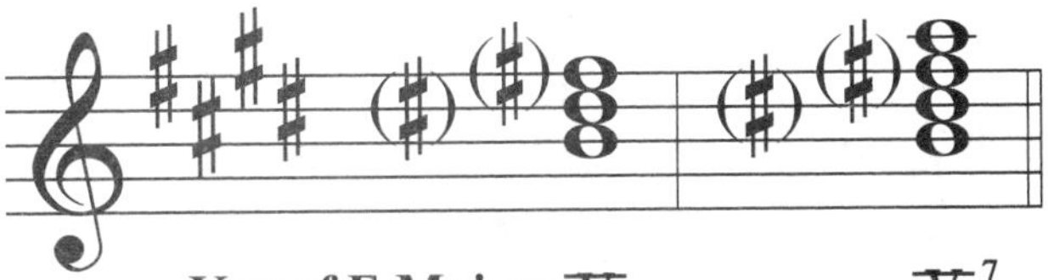

Key of E Major: V **V**^{7}

1. Draw a Dominant 7th chord in each of the following Major keys. The first one is given.

a. Draw the V chord (Dominant).
b. Draw a note that is a minor 7th above the root.

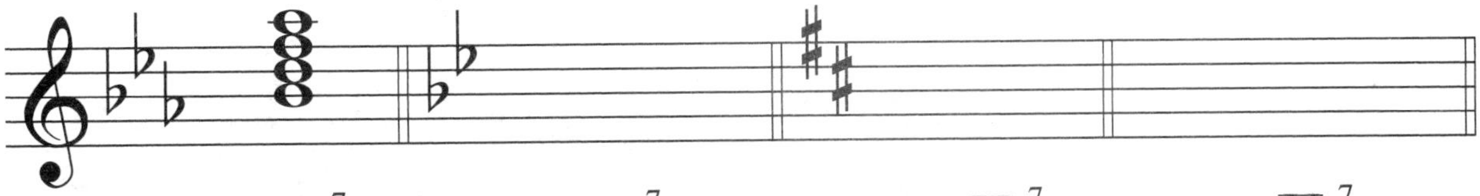

V^{7} V^{7} V^{7} V^{7}

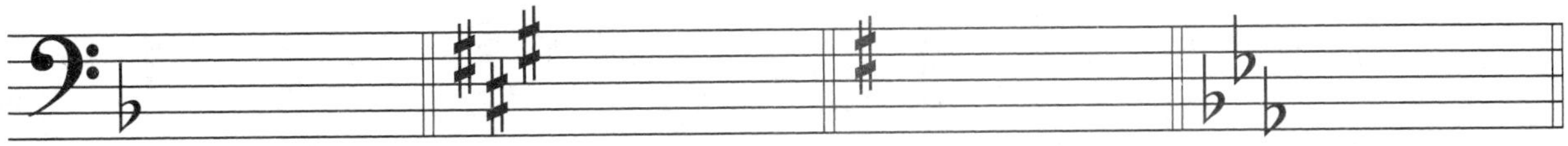

V^{7} V^{7} V^{7} V^{7}

2. Draw a Dominant 7th chord on each of these roots. The first one is given.

a. Complete a Major triad above the given note. b. Add a note that is a minor 7th above the root.

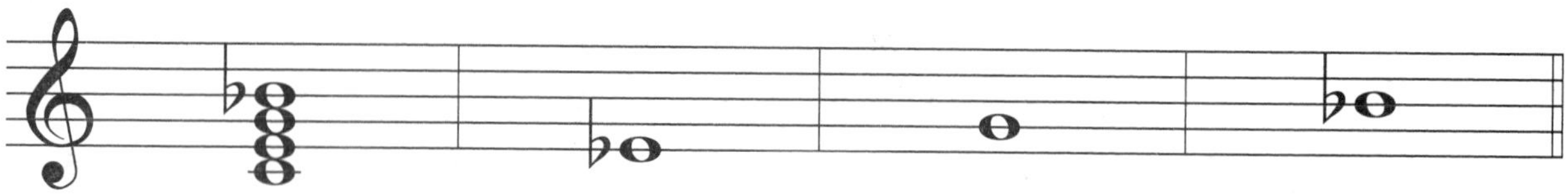

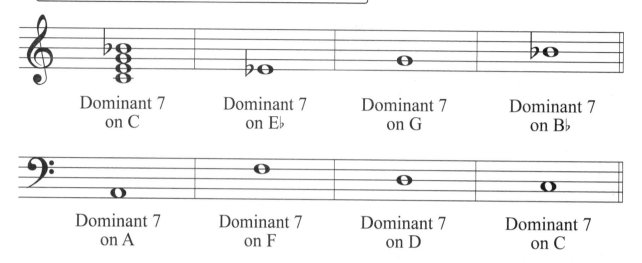

Dominant 7 on C | Dominant 7 on E♭ | Dominant 7 on G | Dominant 7 on B♭

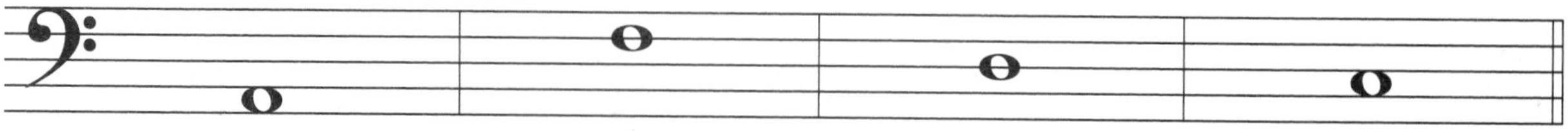

Dominant 7 on A | Dominant 7 on F | Dominant 7 on D | Dominant 7 on C

3. Name the Major key for each of the following examples. Find and circle the Dominant 7th chord(s) in each.

• The root for each Dominant 7th chord will be the fifth note of the key. • Each Dominant 7th chord will have four different notes.

a. Key of _____ Major

b. Key of _____ Major

c. Key of _____ Major

d. Key of _____ Major

LESSON 11
AUTHENTIC, HALF, AND PLAGAL CADENCES

A **CADENCE** is a closing or ending for a musical phrase, made up of a combination of chords. There are many types of cadences. Three common cadences are:

AUTHENTIC, HALF, AND PLAGAL CADENCES

An **AUTHENTIC CADENCE** consists of a V or V^7 chord followed by a I chord:

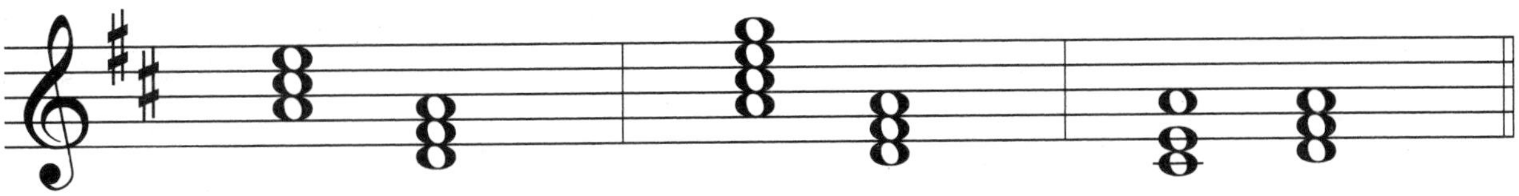

V I V^7 I V^6 I

1. a. Draw authentic cadences using V - I in these keys. Label the chords with Roman numerals. Do not use key signatures. Draw sharps or flats before the notes. The first one is given.

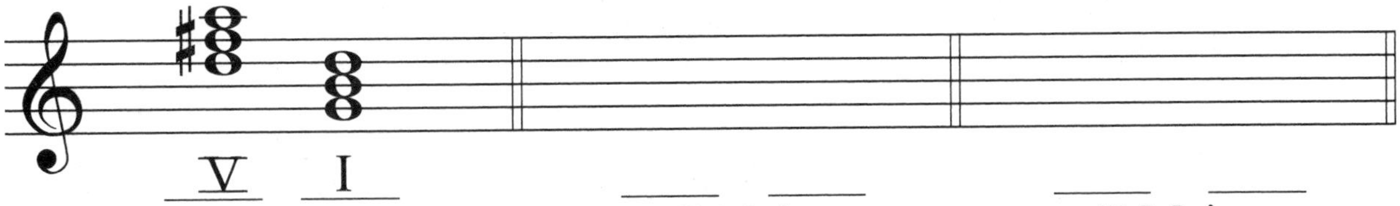

V I ____ ____ ____ ____

G Major C Major E Major

b. Draw authentic cadences using V^7- I in these keys. Label the chords with Roman numerals. Do not use key signatures. Draw sharps or flats before the notes.

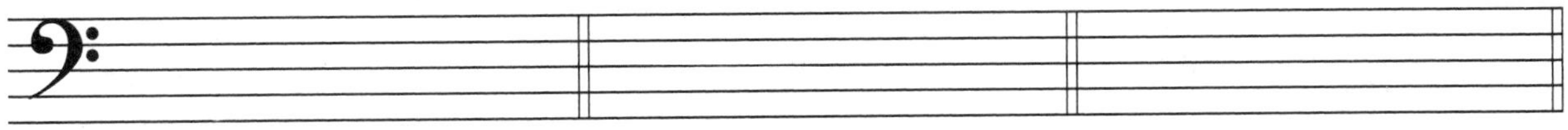

____ ____ ____ ____ ____ ____

D Major A Major F Major

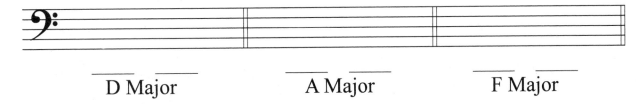

A **PLAGAL CADENCE** consists of a IV chord followed by a I chord:

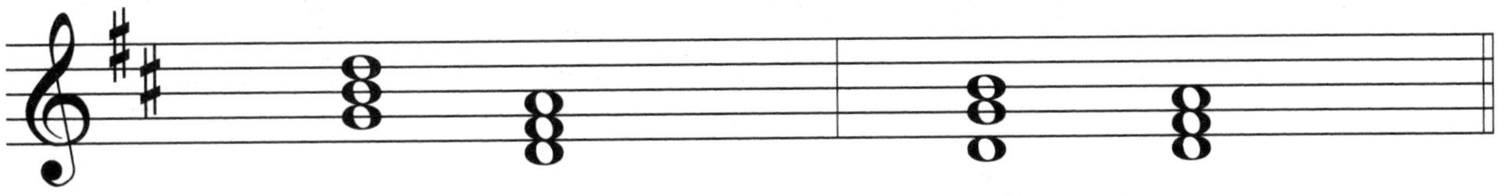

IV I IV_4^6 I

2. Draw plagal cadences in these keys. Label the chords with Roman numerals. Do not use key signatures. Draw sharps or flats before the notes. The first one is given.

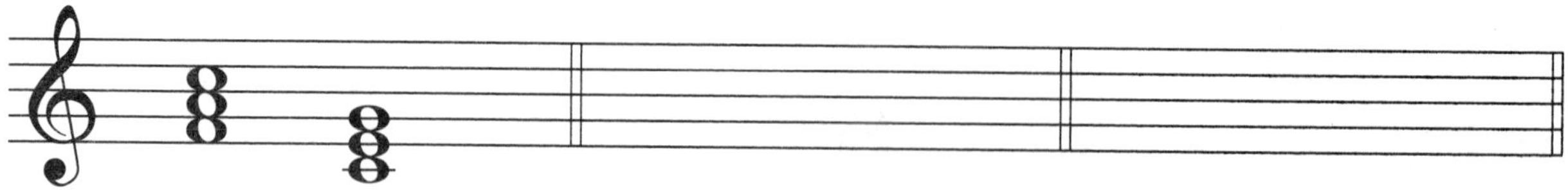

IV I	____ ____	____ ____
C Major	E Major	G Major

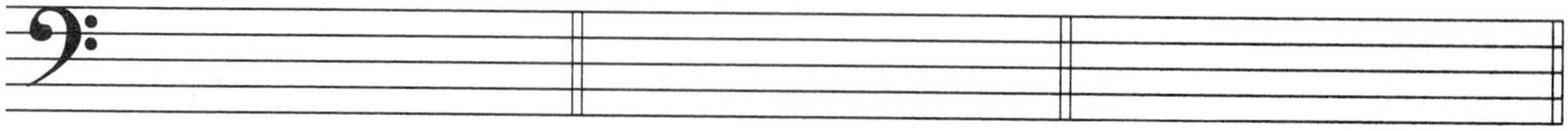

____ ____	____ ____	____ ____
F Major	A Major	D Major

A **HALF CADENCE** is any cadence that ends with a V chord:

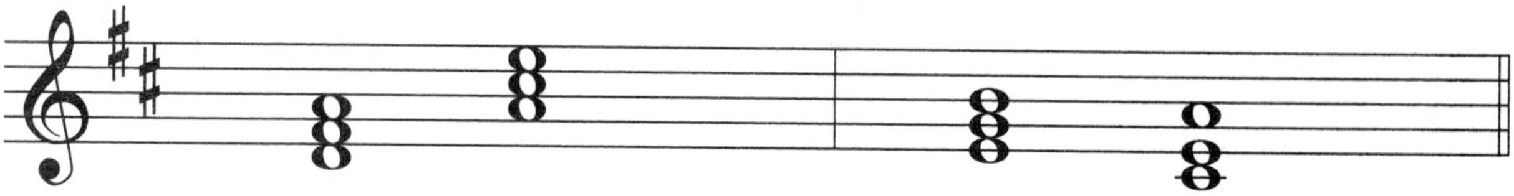

I V ii V^6

3. Draw half cadences using I - V in these keys. Label the chords with Roman numerals. Do not use key signatures. Draw sharps or flats before the notes. The first one is given.

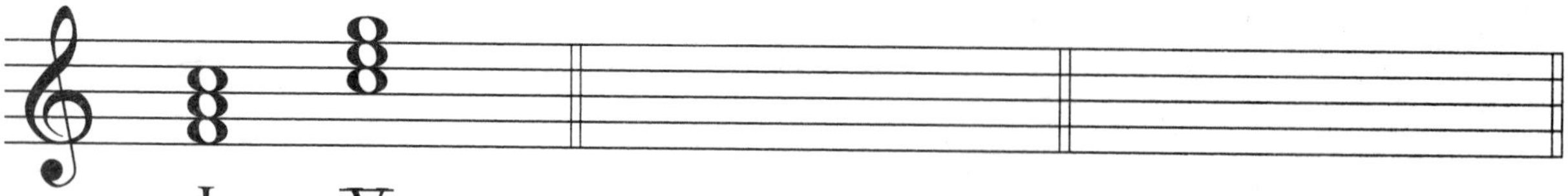

I V	____ ____	____ ____
F Major	A Major	C Major

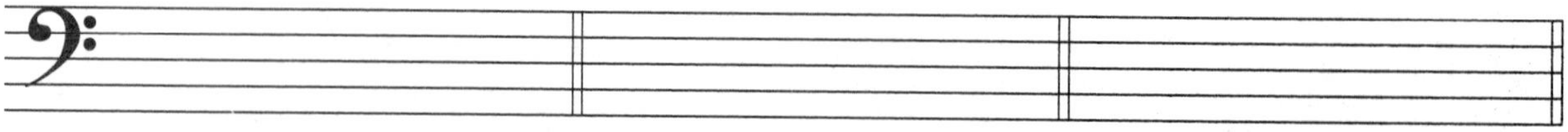

____ ____	____ ____	____ ____
E Major	D Major	G Major

4. Label each of the following chords with Roman numerals and inversions. Name the cadence that is formed by each pair of chords (Authentic, Half, or Plagal). The first one is given.

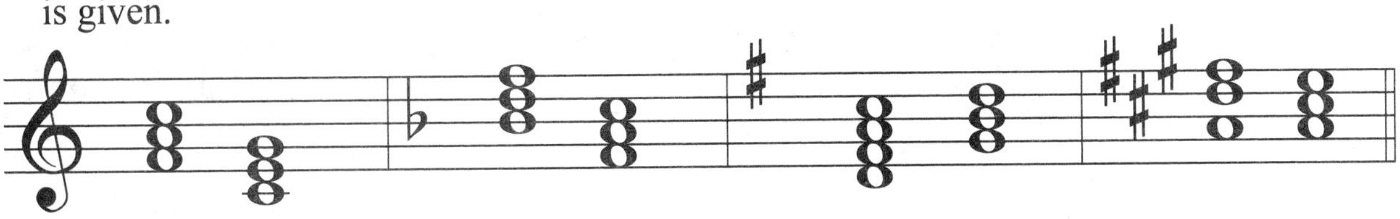

IV I ______ ______ ______ ______ ______ ______

Plagal ____________ ____________ ____________

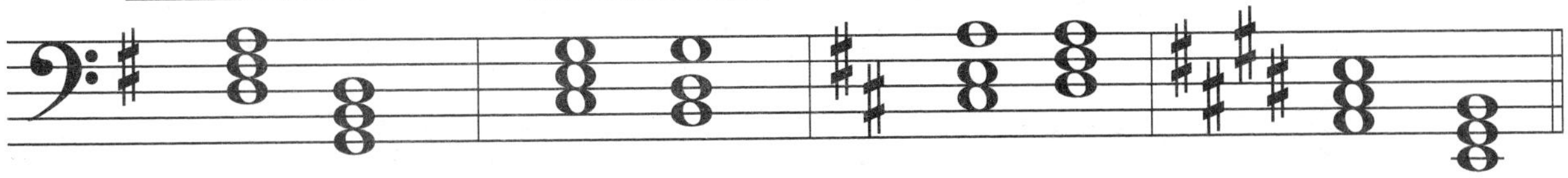

______ ______ ______ ______ ______ ______ ______ ______

____________ ____________ ____________ ____________

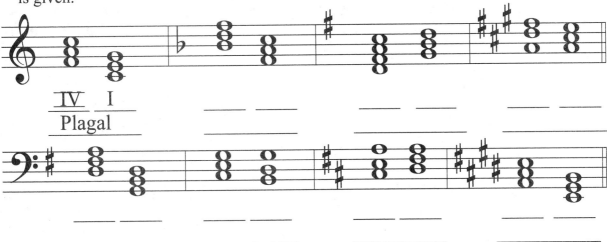

To name cadences in a composition, label the last two chords of the phrase with Roman numerals. These are the two chords that form the cadence.

Example (From *Polonaise in g minor* by J.S. Bach)

V I (Authentic)

5. Name the Major or minor key for each of the following examples. Label each boxed chord with its Roman numeral. Name the cadence formed by the two chords.

a. From *Sonatina: Rondo* by Beethoven. Key of ______ ____________

Roman numerals: ______ ______

Type of Cadence: ____________

b. From *Sonatina* by Beethoven. Key of _____ _______________

Roman numerals: _____ _____
Type of Cadence: ___________

c. From *Hunting Song* by Schumann. Key of _____ _______________

Roman numerals: _____ _____
Type of Cadence: _______________

d. From Humming Song by Schumann. Key of _____ _______________

Roman numerals: _____ _____
Type of Cadence: _______________

REVIEW
WORDS USED IN LESSONS 1-11

Study these words before doing **Review: Lessons 1-11.**

1. **Authentic Cadence:** a cadence made up of the V or V7 chord followed by the I chord (V-I or V7-I)

2. **Cadence:** a closing or ending for a phrase of music, made up of two or more chords

3. **Dominant 7th:** a chord built on the 5th note of the scale, with an added note which is a minor 7th above the root; the quality of the bottom 3 notes is a Major triad, with a minor 7th added

4. **First Inversion:** a triad with the third (or middle) note as the lowest note

5. **Half Cadence:** a cadence which ends with the V chord

6. **Interval:** the distance between two notes, named with numbers and quality

7. **Inversion:** a triad written in a position other than root position; the note which names it is not lowest

8. **Key Signature:** the sharps or flats at the beginning of a composition; there are Major and minor key signatures

9. **Plagal Cadence:** a cadence made up of the IV chord followed by the I chord (IV-I)

10. **Primary Triads:** the I, IV, and V chords; in minor, i, iv, and V

11. **Root Position:** a triad written in a position so that the note which names it is lowest

12. **Scale:** an organized sequence of notes upon which the music is based; scales have the sharps or flats from the key signature with the same name

13. **Scale Degree Names:** Tonic (I), Supertonic (ii), Mediant (iii), Subdominant (IV), Dominant (V), Submediant (vi), Leading Tone (vii°)

14. **Second Inversion:** a triad written with the fifth (or top) note as the lowest note

15. **Secondary Triads:** the ii, iii, vi, and vii° chords; in minor, ii°, III or III^{+}, VI, and vii°

16. **Triad:** a chord with three different notes in it, based on the interval of a third

REVIEW: LESSONS 1-11

1. a. Name these Major keys.

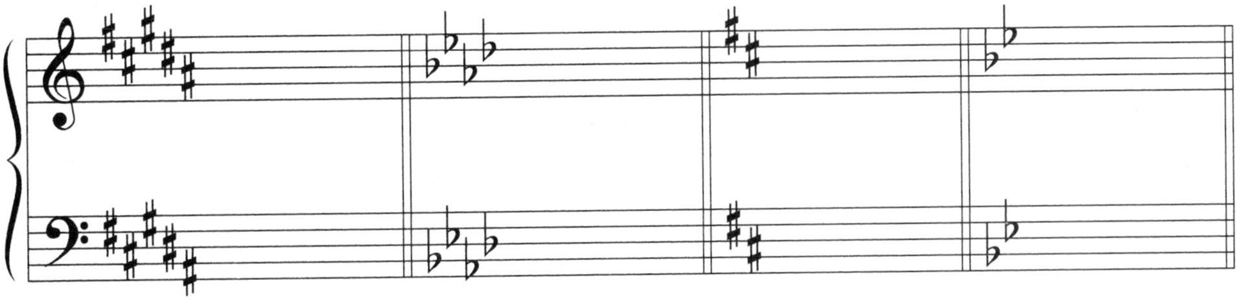

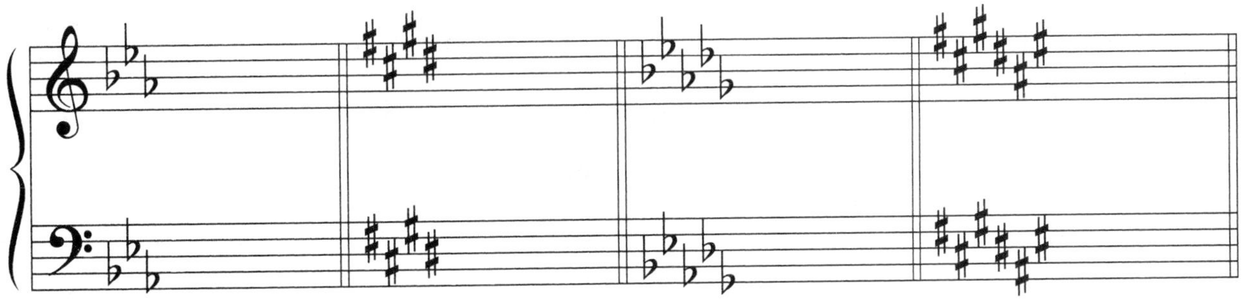

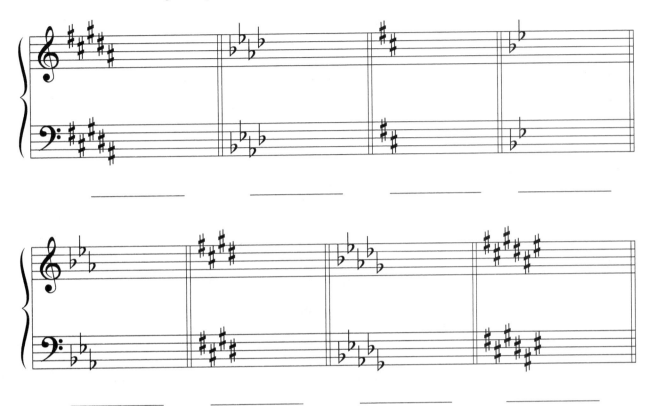

b. Name these minor keys.

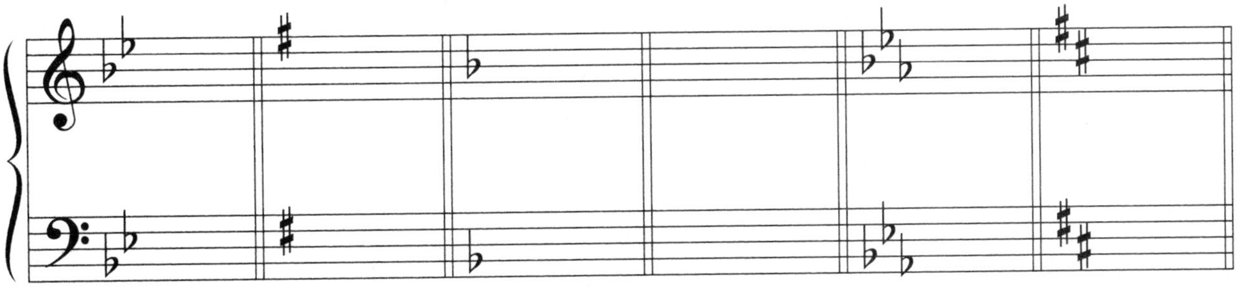

2. Draw the key signatures for these keys in both clefs.

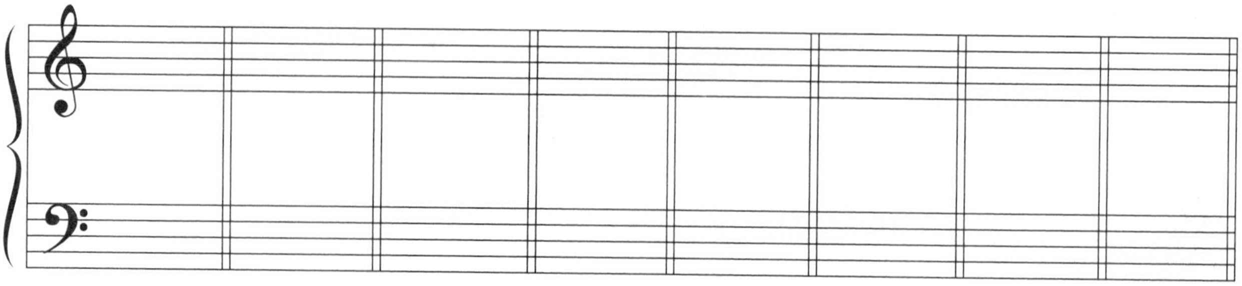

E Major F Major E♭ Major A Major D Major G Major G♭ Major C♯ Major

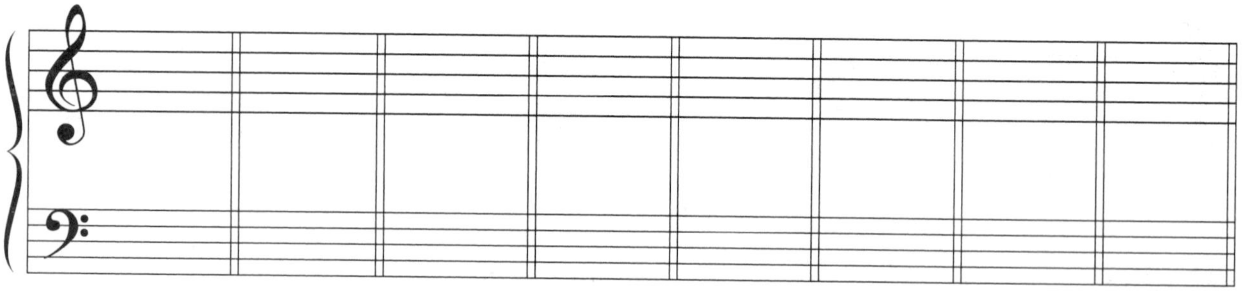

B♭ Major a minor g minor c minor e minor d minor b minor D♭ Major

3. Draw these scales.

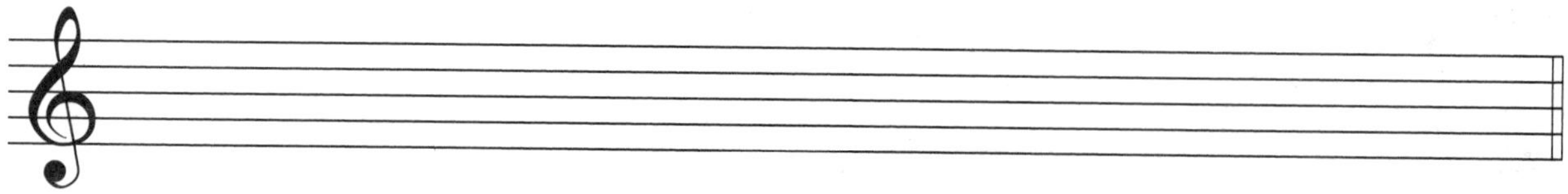

D Major

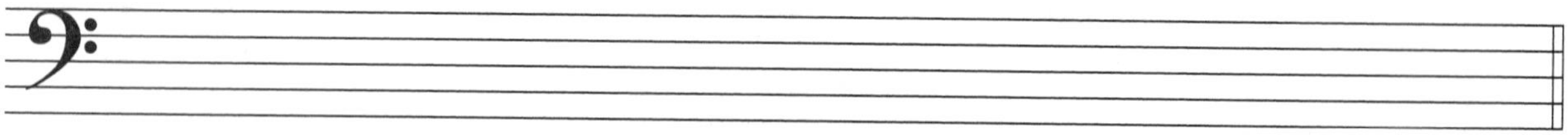

B♭ Major

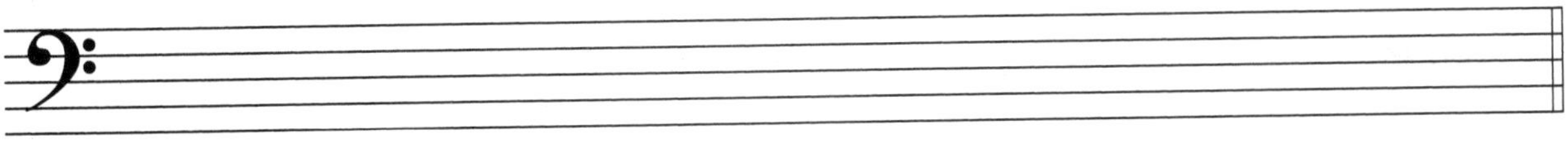

c natural minor

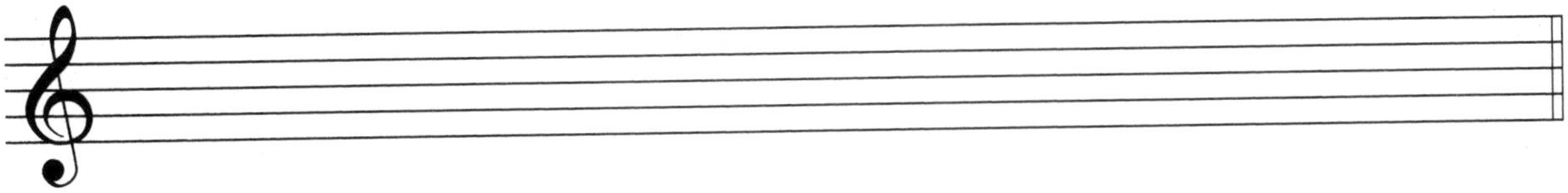

g harmonic minor

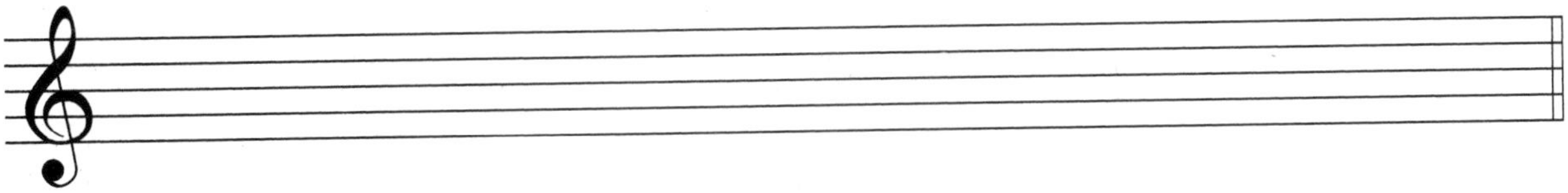

b harmonic minor

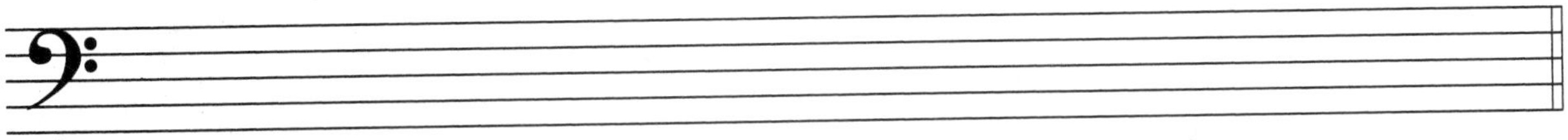

G♭ Major

4. Label these chords with their roots, qualities (Major, minor, diminished, or Dominant 7th), and inversions. The first one is given.

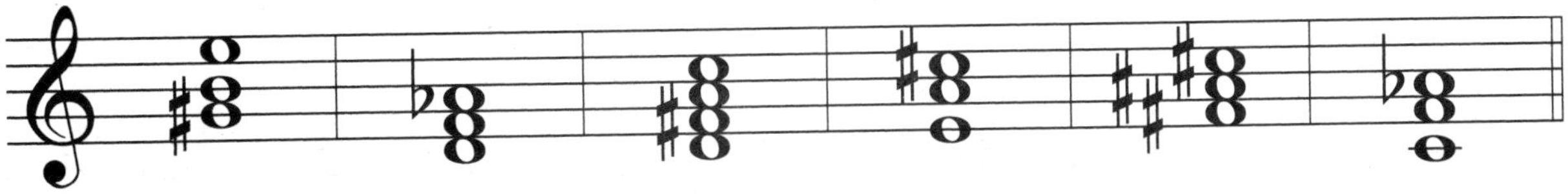

E Major [6] ____________ ____________ ____________ ____________ ____________

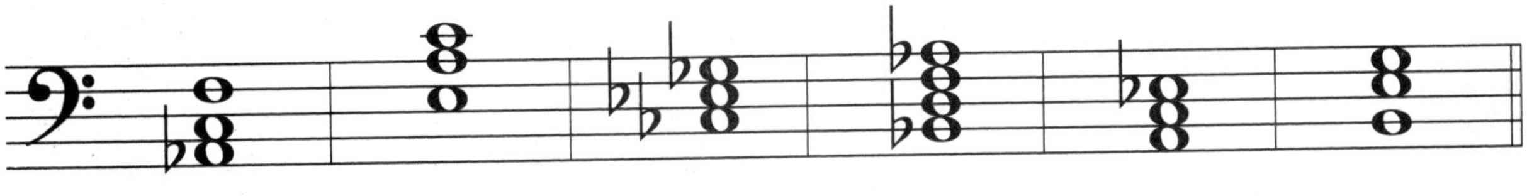

____________ ____________ ____________ ____________ ____________ ____________

5. Draw these triads.

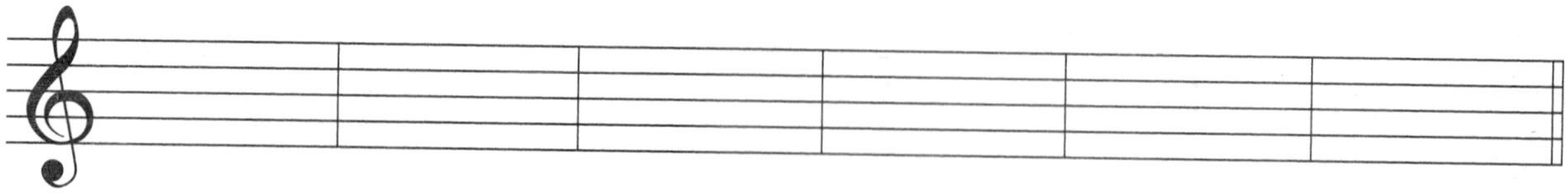

C♯ Major | d♭ minor $^{5}_{3}$ | Dom.^{7} on F | D Major ^{6} | g♭ minor | G Major $^{6}_{3}$

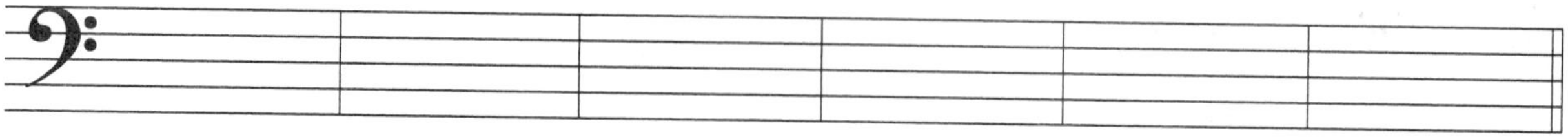

E Major $^{6}_{3}$ | d minor $^{6}_{4}$ | g minor ^{6} | $\underline{\text{V}}^{7}$ in the key of A Major | a minor $^{6}_{4}$ | e minor ^{6}

6. Name these intervals with their qualities and numbers. The first one is given.

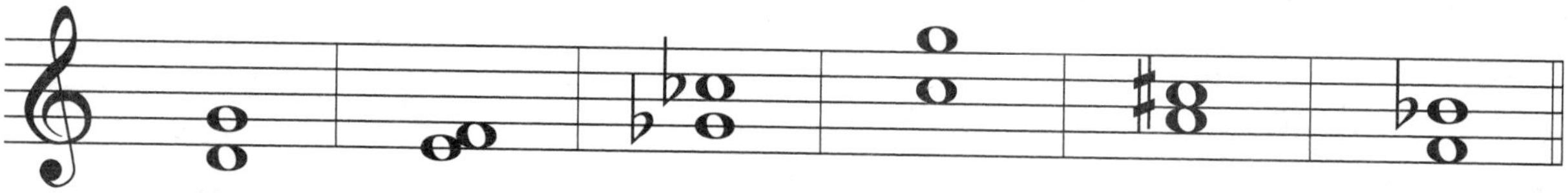

P4

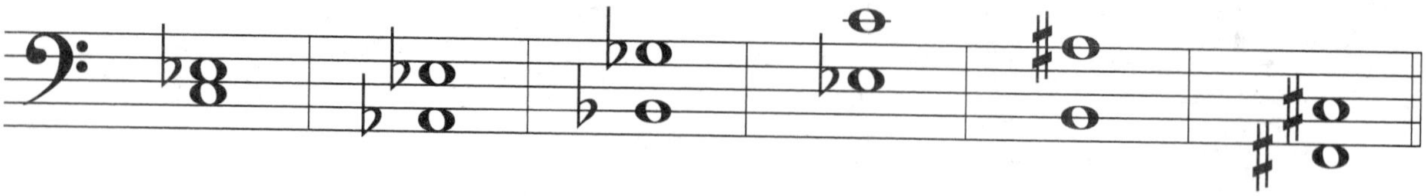

7. Draw a note above each given note to complete these intervals. The first one is given.

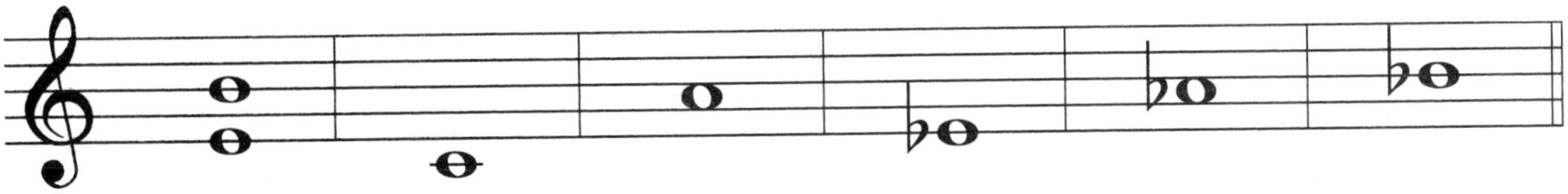

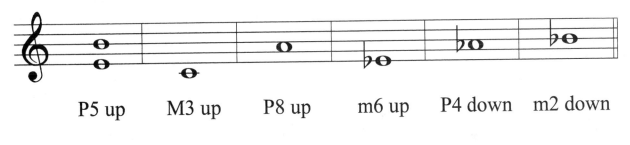

P5 up   M3 up   P8 up   m6 up   P4 down   m2 down

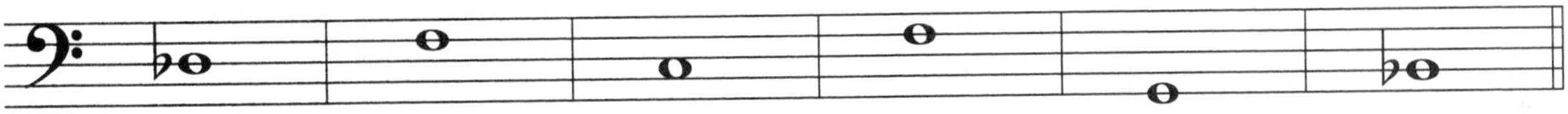

m7 up   M2 down   M6 down   m3 down   m6 up   M7 up

8. Match these scale degree names with their Roman numerals.

_____	Dominant 7th	a. IV
_____	Dominant	b. iii
_____	Subdominant	c. V
_____	Leading Tone	d. vii°
_____	Mediant	e. ii
_____	Submediant	f. I
_____	Supertonic	g. vi
_____	Tonic	h. V^7

9. The following example is from a Sonatina by Beethoven. Answer the questions about the music.

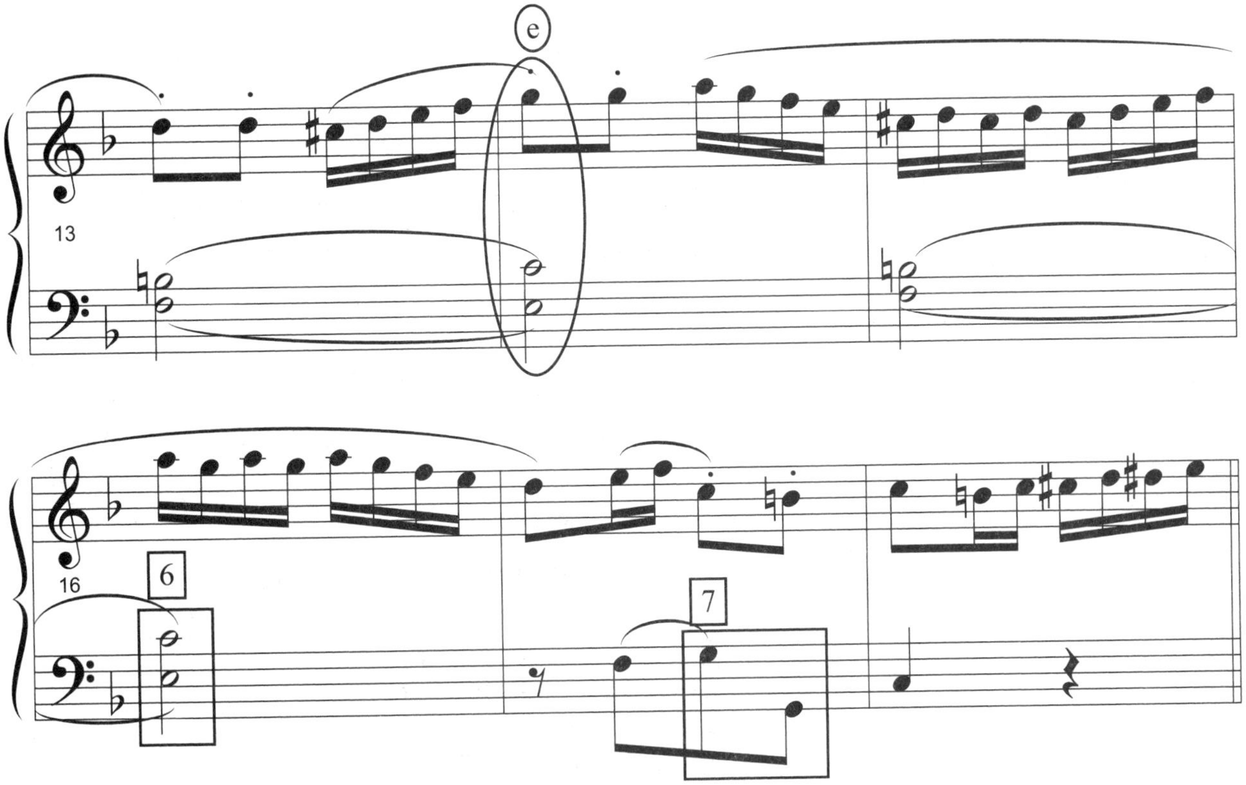

a. What is the key or tonality? _____ _______________

b. What scale is used in measure 2? _____ _______________

c. Name each circled chord with its root, quality, Roman numeral, and inversion. Draw lines above and below the Roman numerals for Major chords. The first one is given.

	ROOT	QUALITY	ROMAN NUMERAL AND INV.
Triad a.	F	Major	I (I^5_3)
Triad b.	________	________	________
Triad c.	________	________	________
Triad d.	________	________	________
Triad e.	________	________	________

d. Name each boxed interval with its quality and number. The first one is given.

1. m2 2. ______ 3. ______ 4. ______ 5. ______ 6. ______ 7. ______

e. Name the cadence in measures 3-4. ____________________

Name the cadence in measures 7-8. ____________________

10. The following example is from *First Loss* by Schumann. Answer the questions about the music.

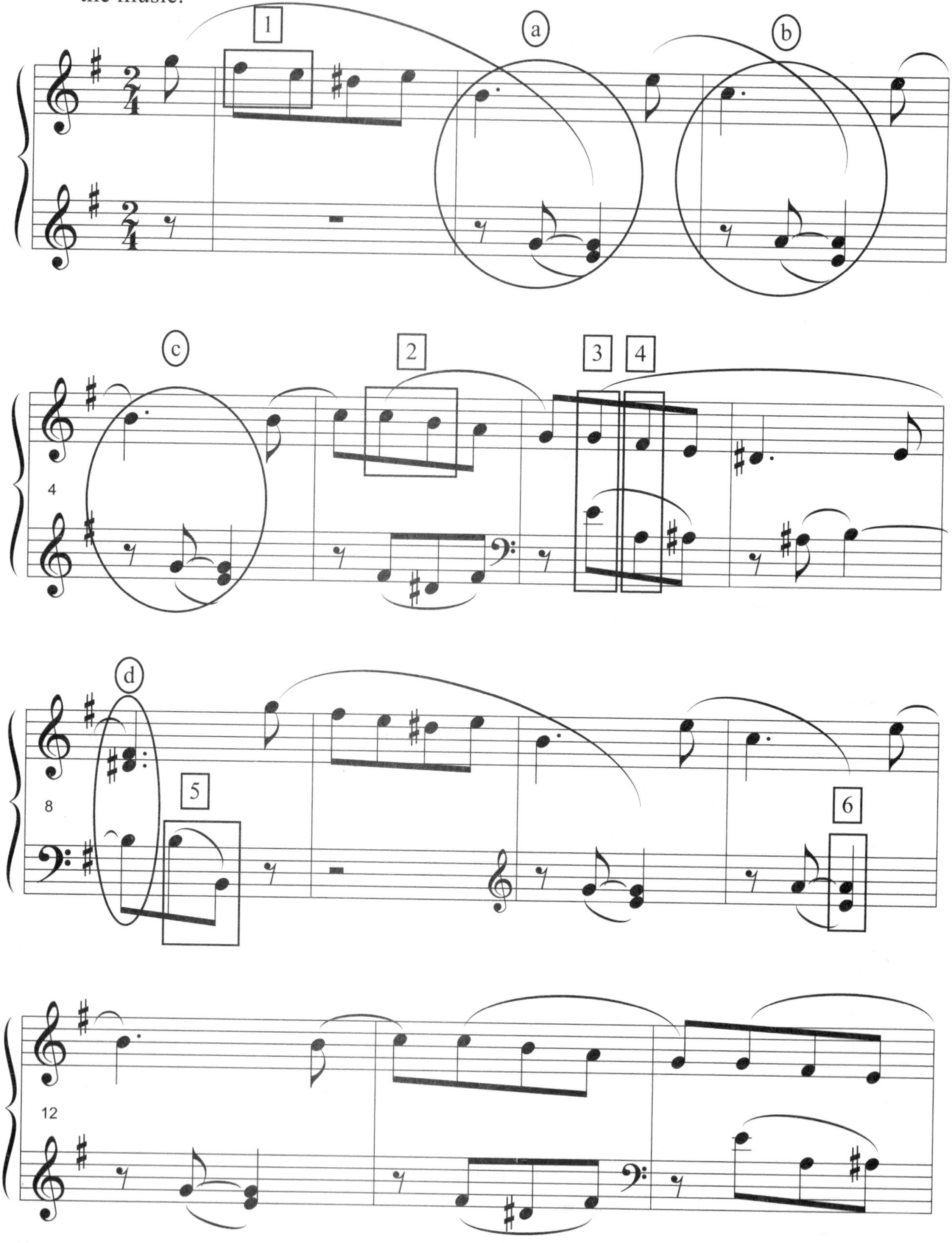

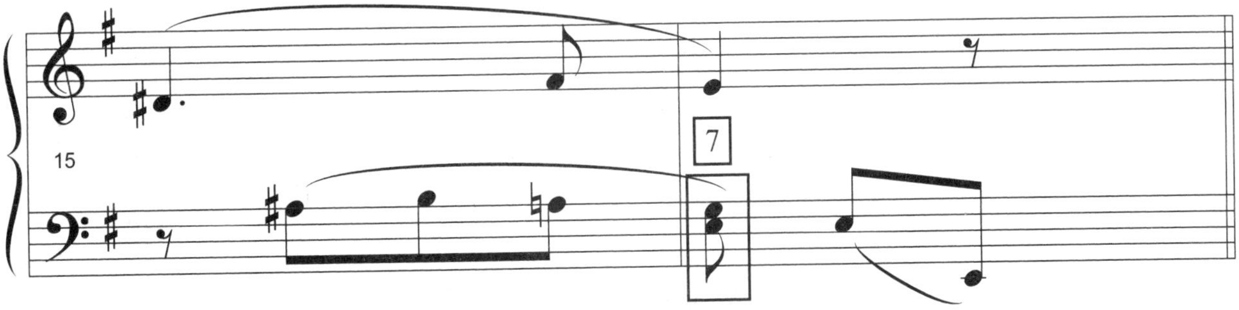

a. What is the minor key or tonality? _____ ________________

b. Which form of minor is used? (Circle the answer.)

Natural Harmonic

c. Name each circled chord with its root, quality, and inversion. The first one is given.

	ROOT	QUALITY	INVERSION
Triad a.	e	minor	$^{5}_{3}$ or R
Triad b.			
Triad c.			
Triad d.			

d. Does the note A♯ belong to this key? (Yes or no.) ___________

e. Name each boxed interval with its quality and number. The first one is given.

1. M2 2. ______ 3. ______ 4. ______ 5. ______ 6. ______ 7. ______

f. What type of cadence is used in measures 7-8? (Circle the answer.)

Authentic Half

g. What type of cadence is used in measures 15-16? (Circle the answer.)

Authentic Half

11. The following example is from a Polonaise by J.S. Bach. Answer the questions about the music.

a. What is the minor key or tonality? _____ ______________

b. Which form of minor is used? (Circle the answer.)

Natural Harmonic

c. To which Major key does the music change in measure 9? _____ ______________

d. How are these two keys related? (Circle the answer.)

Parallel Relative

e. Name each circled chord with its root, quality, and inversion. The first one is given.

	ROOT	QUALITY	INVERSION
Triad a.	g	minor	$^6_3$ (or ^{6} or 1st)
Triad b.	______	______	______
Triad c.	______	______	______
Triad d.	______	______	______

f. Name each boxed interval with its quality and number. The first one is given.

1. m2 2. ______ 3. ______ 4. ______ 5. ______ 6. ______ 7. ______

g. What type of cadence is used in measures 3-4? ______________

h. What type of cadence is used in measure 8? ______________

This page has purposely been left blank.

LESSON 12
TIME SIGNATURES

The **TIME SIGNATURE** is found at the beginning of the music, to the right of the key signature. The time signature is typically made up of two numbers:

Sometimes, the letter 𝄴 or 𝄵 is used instead of numbers.

𝄴 stands for 4/4 or **Common Time.**

𝄵 stands for 2/2 or ***alla breve.***

The **top** number of the time signature tells **how many beats each measure receives.**

The **bottom** number tells **which type of note receives one beat.**

2 = 2 beats or counts per measure
4 = Quarter note (♩) receives one beat or count

3 = 3 beats or counts per measure
8 = Eighth note (♪) receives one beat or count

METER is the arrangement of beats into equal size (measures) and with regular recurring accents, such as three beats per measure in 3/4.

When the bottom number of a time signature is 4, a quarter note (♩) receives one beat. The following chart shows two types of counting. Other forms of counting are possible.

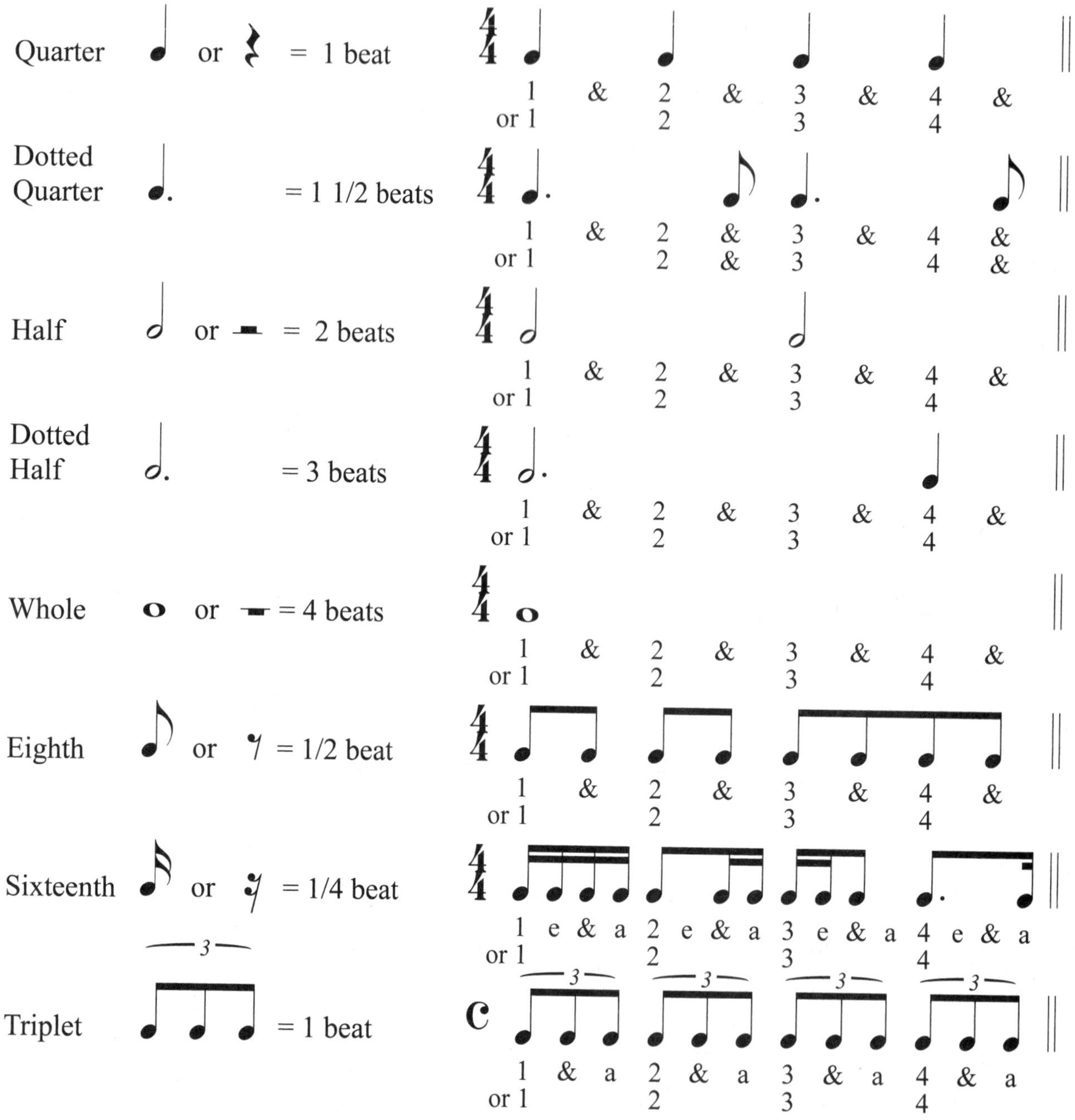

An **UPBEAT** occurs when the music begins with an incomplete measure. The last beat or beats are "borrowed" from the final measure and placed at the beginning. The counts in the upbeat measure are the last numbers of the time signature. The final measure will have fewer beats than normal. The first full measure begins with count number 1.

Example: 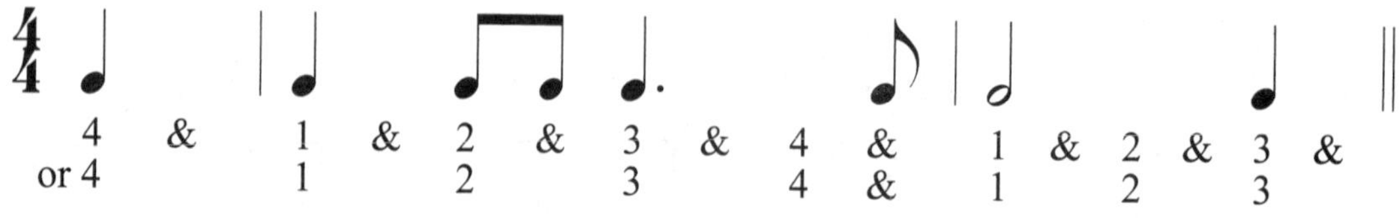

In $\frac{2}{4}$ the first beat of each measure is strongest. There are two equal beats per measure.*

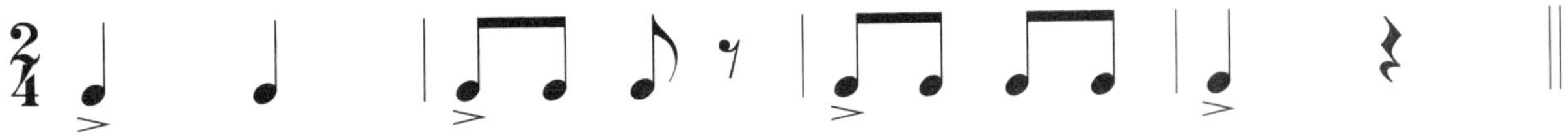

In $\frac{3}{4}$ the first beat of each measure is strongest. There are three equal beats per measure.

In $\frac{4}{4}$ the first beat of each measure is strongest. The third beat is also a strong beat, but not as strong as beat one. There are four equal beats per measure.

1. Fill in the blanks. The first one is given.

2 = 2 beats per measure. The first beat is strongest.
4 = Quarter note receives one beat.

3 = ______________________________
4 = ______________________________

4 = ______________________________
4 = ______________________________

C stands for ______________________________

¢ stands for ______________________________

5 = ______________________________
4 = ______________________________

7 = ______________________________
4 = ______________________________

*The accents in these rhythm patterns are only intended to demonstrate strong beats and weak beats within the meter. They are not meant to imply that every strong beat receives an accent.

2. Write counts between the clefs for each of the following phrases. Draw accents on the strong beats. The first measure is given.

a. From *Allegro Scherzando* by Haydn.

b. From *Polonaise in g minor* by J.S. Bach.

c. From *Shepherd Playing on His Pipe, Op. 31,* by Rebikov.

d. From *Arabesque* by Burgmuller.

e. From *Elfin Dance* by Grieg.

When the bottom number of a time signature is 2, a half note (𝅗𝅥) receives one beat. The following chart shows two types of counting. Other forms of counting are possible.

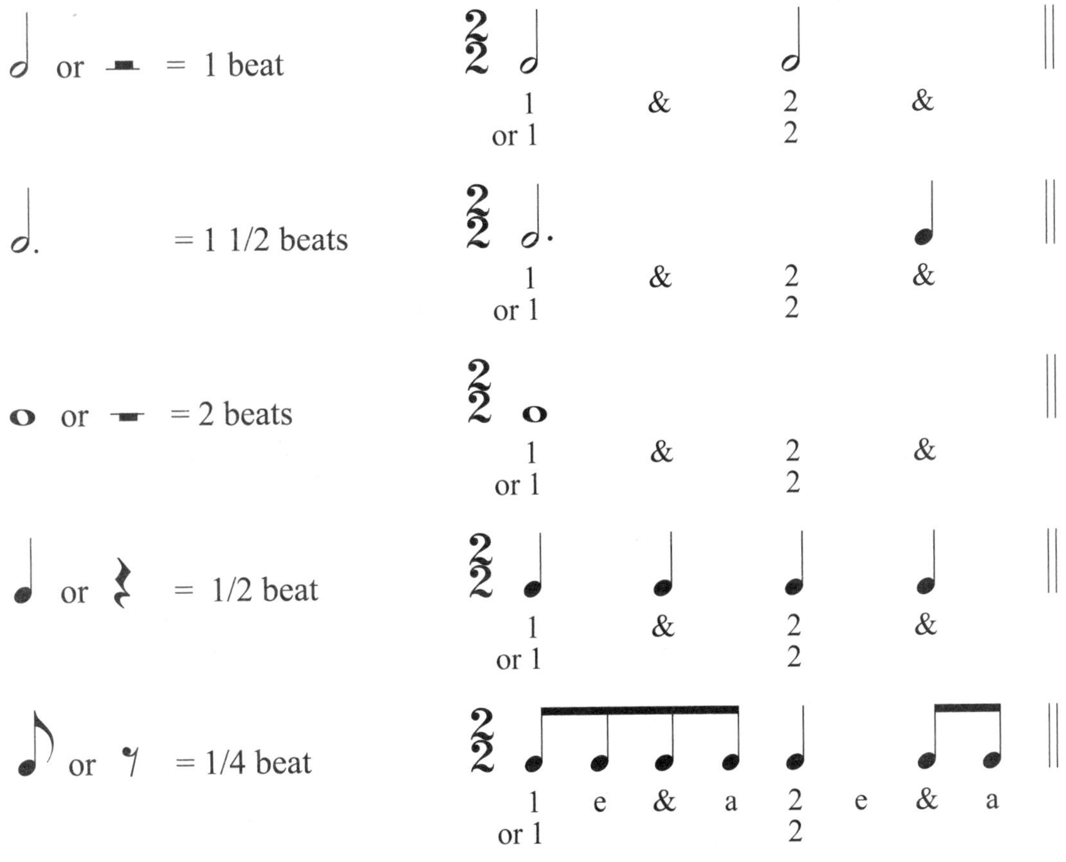

In $\frac{2}{2}$ the first beat of each measure is strongest. There are two equal beats per measure.

An 8 as the bottom number of a time signature indicates that an eighth note (𝅘𝅥𝅮) receives one beat. However, time signatures with a bottom number of 8 have basic beats of a dotted quarter note (♩.). $\frac{6}{8}$ has two pulses per measure. Two forms of counting are shown.

𝅘𝅥𝅯 or 𝄿 = 1/2 beat

𝅘𝅥𝅮 or 𝄾 = 1 beat

♩ or 𝄽 = 2 beats

♩. or = 3 beats

𝅗𝅥. or 𝄻 = 6 beats

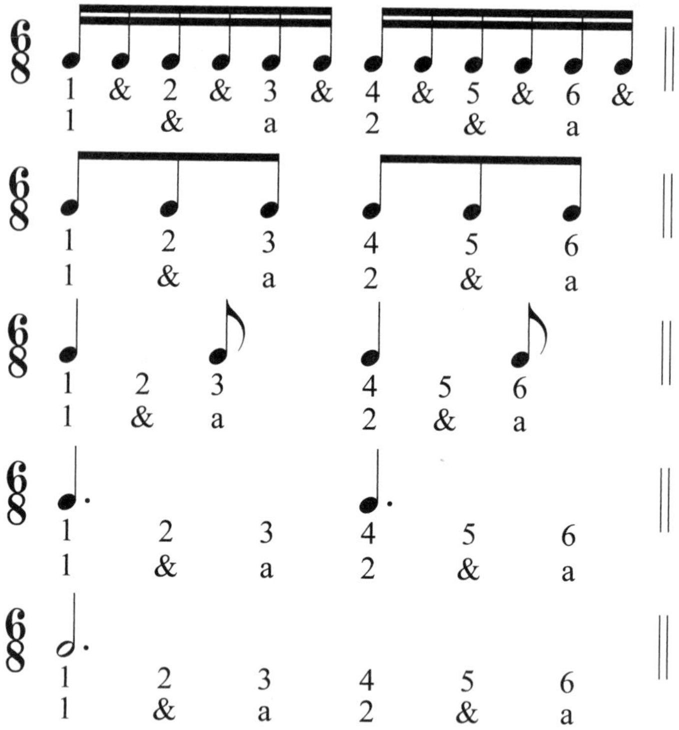

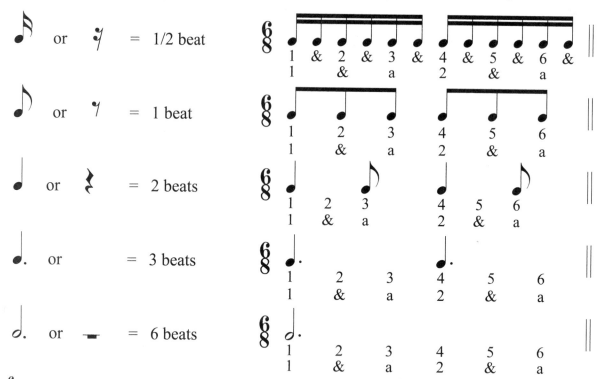

In $\frac{6}{8}$ the first beat of each measure is strongest. Beat four is also a strong beat, but not as strong as beat one.

3. Fill in the blanks.

$\frac{6}{8}$ = ______ beats in a measure.
= eighth note (𝅘𝅥𝅮) receives ______ beat.

$\frac{9}{8}$ = 9 beats in a ________________.
= ________________ receives one beat.

$\frac{12}{8}$ = ______ beats in a measure.
= ______________ receives one beat.

$\frac{2}{2}$ = 2 beats in a ______________.
= ________________ receives one beat.

$\frac{3}{2}$ = _______ beats in a measure.
= Half note receives ________________.

$\frac{12}{2}$ = _________________________ in a measure.
= _________________________ receives one beat.

4. Write counts between the clefs for each of the following phrases. Draw accents on the strong beats.

a. From *Ballade* by Burgmuller.

b. From *Hunting Song* by Schumann.

c. From *Bouree No. 1* by Kirnberger.

d. From *Sonatina, Op. 55, No. 1: Vivace*, by Kuhlau.

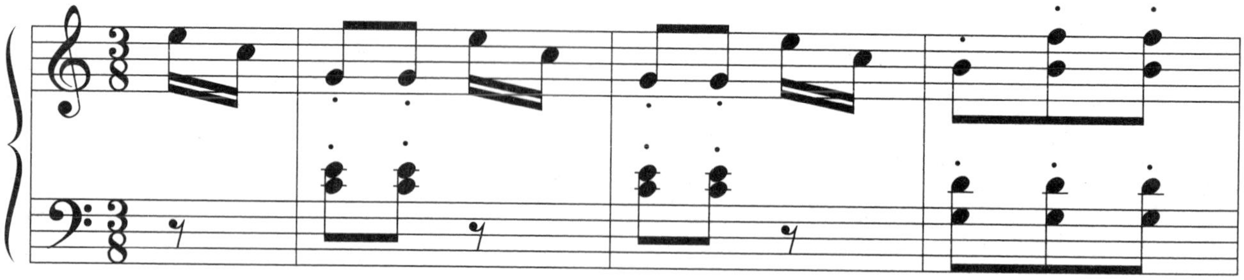

5. Circle the correct time signature for each of the following rhythm patterns.

- In $\frac{3}{4}$ the eighth notes will occur in groups of two or four.
- In $\frac{6}{8}$ the eighth notes will occur in groups of three.

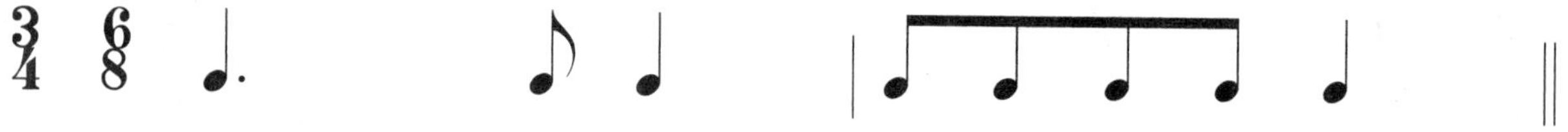

LESSON 13
SIGNS AND TERMS

The following performance terms and symbols may appear in music you are studying.

a tempo: return to the original tempo (the speed at which the music began)

accent: play the note louder than the others

accelerando: accelerate; gradually faster

adagio: slowly

allegro: fast or quick, cheerfully, merrily

allegretto: slightly slower than *allegro;* faster than *andante*

andante: a moderate walking tempo

andantino: slightly faster than *andante;* some composers use it to mean slower than *andante*

arpeggio: a broken chord: 

articulation: the various ways notes are executed, including but not limited to *staccato* and *legato*

cantabile: in a singing style

< ***crescendo (cresc.):*** gradually louder

D.C. al fine: go back to the beginning and play to *fine*

└───┘ or *Ped.* ✻ **damper pedal:** press the pedal on the right

> ***decrescendo (decresc.) or diminuendo (dim.):*** gradually softer

dolce: sweetly

dynamics: letters or symbols that indicate how loud or soft the music should sound

espressivo: expressively

f ***forte:*** loud

ff ***fortissimo:*** very loud

fff ***fortississimo:*** very, very loud

𝄐 ***fermata:*** hold the note longer than its value

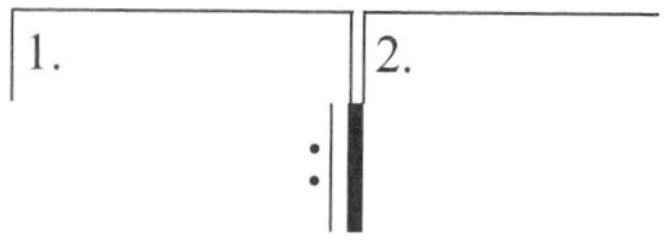

first and second ending: play the music with the first ending (under the 1.), then repeat the music; the second time through, skip the first ending and play the second ending (under the 2.)

legato: play smoothly, connect the notes

***legato* pedal:** also known as syncopated pedal or overlapping pedal, creation of a seamless, unblurred *legato* by raising and quickly re-depressing the damper pedal at the same time as or immediately after the keys are struck

leggiero: lightly, delicately

lento: slowly

mf ***mezzo forte:*** medium loud

mp ***mezzo piano:*** medium soft

moderato: a moderate or medium tempo

molto: much, very

octave sign: play the notes an octave higher (or lower if under the notes) than where they are written

parallel Major and minor: Major and minor keys with the same letter names (such as C Major and c minor)

p ***piano:*** soft

pp ***pianissimo:*** very soft

ppp ***pianississimo:*** very, very soft

phrase: a musical sentence, often but not always four measures long

presto: very fast

poco: little

rallentando: gradually slower

repeat sign: repeat the music; go back to the nearest repeat signs, or to the beginning of the music if there are none

ritardando (ritard., rit.): gradually slower

sfz or ***sf*** or ***fz*** ***sforzando:*** a sudden sharp accent

slur: curved line indicating to play *legato*

spiritoso: spirited; with spirit

staccato: play crisply or detached

tenuto: hold the note for its full value; may also mean to stress the note

subito: suddenly; at once

tempo: the speed at which to play the music

tie: hold the second note, do not repeat it

tre corde (t.c.): release the *una corda* pedal (the left pedal)

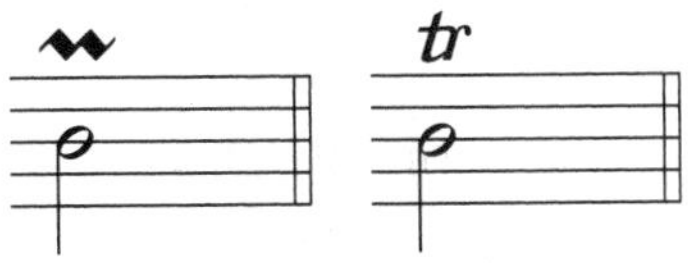

trill: Alternate between the written note and the note below the written note. In music of the Baroque or Classical Periods (see Lesson 16), the trill is typically performed beginning on the note above the written note, as in example A. In the Romantic Period the trill typically begins on the written note, as in example B.*

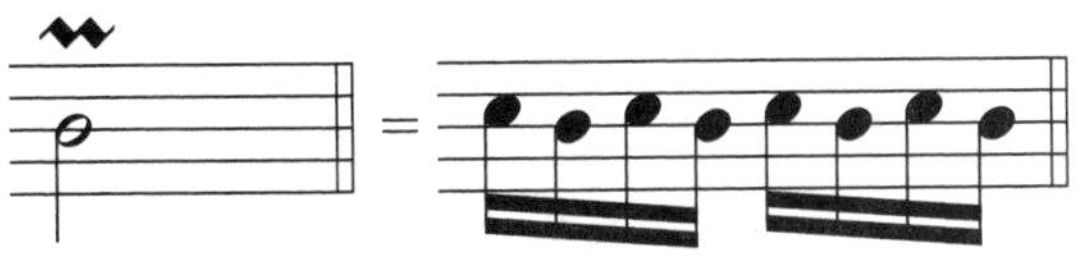

A. Classical Period

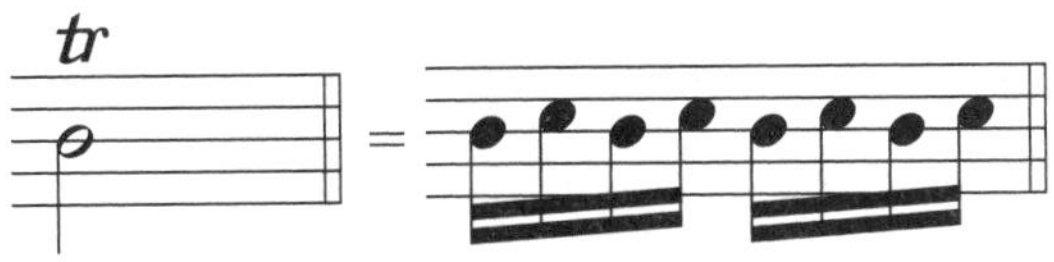

B. Romantic Period

una corda (u.c.): press the left pedal (the soft pedal)

vivace: quick, lively

-------***etto:*** suffix meaning little

-------***ino:*** suffix meaning little

*The trill may be interpreted differently depending on the historical period and the context of the music. Further study of ornamentation is encouraged.

1. Match these terms and symbols with their definitions.

_____ *mf* a. *mezzo piano:* medium soft

_____ *ff* b. *pianissimo:* very soft

_____ *mp* c. *piano:* soft

_____ *p* d. *fortissimo:* very loud

_____ *f* e. *mezzo forte*: medium loud

_____ *pp* f. symbols that indicate loud or soft

_____ dynamics g. *forte:* loud

_____ *fff* h. play the notes an octave higher than written

_____ *ppp* i. *fortississimo:* very, very loud

_____ 8*va* j. *sforzando:* a sudden, sharp accent

_____ *sfz* k. *pianississimo:* very, very soft

2. Match these terms and symbols with their definitions.

_____ 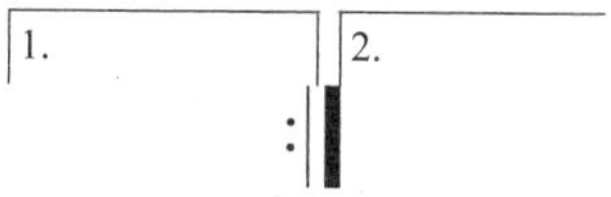

a. play smoothly, connect the notes

_____  b. repeat sign: repeat the music

_____  c. suffix meaning little

_____ *legato* d. curved line indicating to play *legato*

_____ ------ino e. *fermata:* hold the note longer than its value

_____ 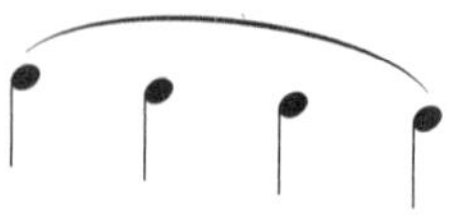 f. first and second ending

_____  g. *staccato:* detached

3. Match these terms and symbols with their definitions.

_____ 

_____ 

_____ phrase

_____ Ped. *

_____ *D.C. al fine*

_____ *ritardando (rit.)*

_____ *a tempo*

a. use the damper pedal (the pedal on the right)

b. a musical sentence, often four measures long

c. hold the note for its full value (or stress the note)

d. accent: play the note louder than the others

e. gradually slower

f. return to the original tempo (the speed at which the music began)

g. go back to the beginning and play until the word *fine*

4. Match these terms and symbols with their definitions.

_____ *allegro*

_____ *andante*

_____ *moderato*

_____ *vivace*

_____ 

_____ 

_____ *adagio*

_____ *lento*

_____ *------etto*

a. a moderate walking tempo

b. gradually louder

c. suffix meaning little

d. gradually softer

e. slowly

f. a moderate or medium tempo

g. quick or lively

h. fast, quick, cheerfully, merrily

i. slowly

5. Match these terms and symbols with their definitions.

_____ *andantino*

_____ *dolce*

_____ *allegretto*

_____ *accelerando*

_____  (Baroque & Classical)

_____ *una corda (u.c.)*

_____ *cantabile*

_____ *molto*

_____ 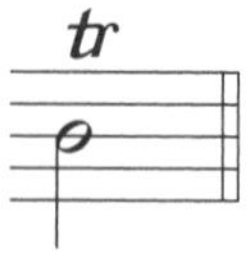 (Romantic)

_____ *poco*

_____ *tre corde (t.c.)*

_____ *spiritoso*

a. trill: 

b. slightly faster than *andante*

c. press the soft pedal (left pedal)

d. slightly slower than *allegro*

e. sweetly

f. gradually faster

g. with spirit

h. little

i. much, greatly

j. release the soft pedal (left pedal)

k. trill: 

l. in a singing style

6. Match these terms and symbols with their definitions.

_____ *presto*

_____ *subito*

_____ *espressivo*

_____ *leggiero*

_____ parallel Major and minor

_____ arpeggio

_____ *legato* pedal

_____ articulation

a. a broken chord

b. expressively

c. lightly, delicately

d. Major and minor keys with same letter names

e. very fast

f. suddenly; at once

g. the manner in which notes are executed, including but not limited to *staccato* and *legato*

h. a seamless *legato* by use of the damper pedal

LESSON 14
TRANSPOSITION

TRANSPOSITION occurs when music is played or written in a key that is different from the original.

Example A is in the key of C Major. Example B is in G Major. The music has been transposed from C Major to G Major.

The intervals remain the same in both versions. The melody sounds the same, but is higher in pitch.

EXAMPLE A: FRERE JACQUES in the key of C Major.

EXAMPLE B: FRERE JACQUES in the key of G Major.

TRANSPOSING A MELODY: METHOD 1

1. Look at the first note of the original melody and determine its scale degree.

G Major: Tonic

2. Draw the first note of the melody in the new key on the correct scale degree. Use the correct rhythm.

D Major: Tonic

3. Name the intervals in the original melody.

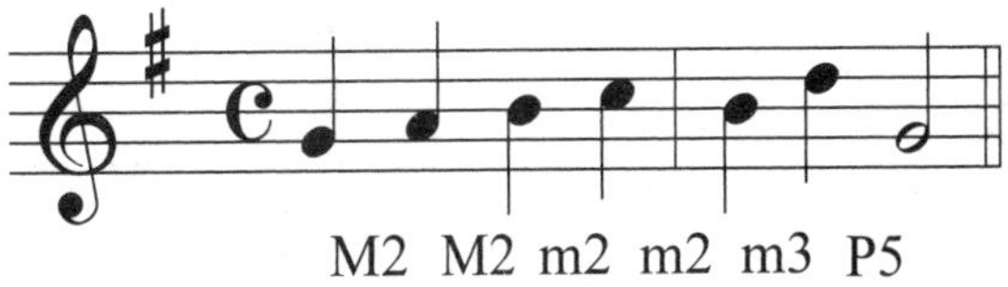

4. Continue the melody in the new key using the same intervals and directions (up or down) that appear in the original melody. Use the correct rhythm.

TRANSPOSING A MELODY: METHOD 1

1. Compare the original key with the new key. Determine the interval between the original key and the new key.

G Major to D Major: P4 down or P5 up

2. Move each note of the original melody the distance of that interval.

G becomes D
A becomes E
B becomes F♯
C becomes G
D becomes A
E becomes B
F♯ becomes C♯

3. Draw the melody in the new key using the correct rhythm and directions

The following example is transposed from C Major to G Major.

Method 1: Each interval is marked, and the transposition is based on the original intervals.

Method 2: Each note is raised a Perfect 5th.

MARY HAD A LITTLE LAMB in C Major

MARY HAD A LITTLE LAMB in G Major

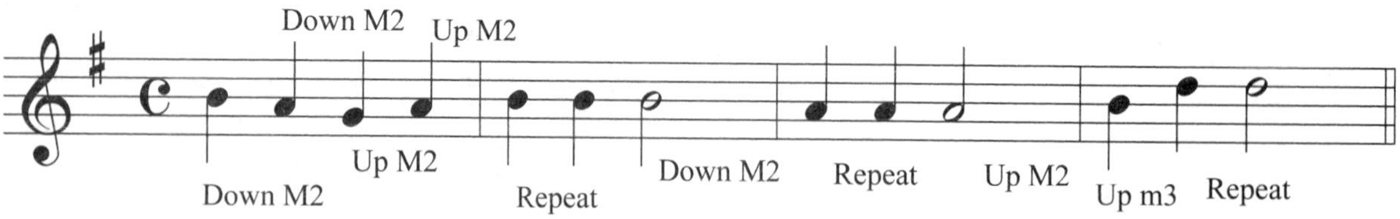

1. Determine the key to which each of these melodies has been transposed.

a. *Long Long Ago:* Original key - C Major

Long Long Ago: Transposed to ____________________

b. *London Bridge:* Original key - G Major

London Bridge: Transposed to ______________________

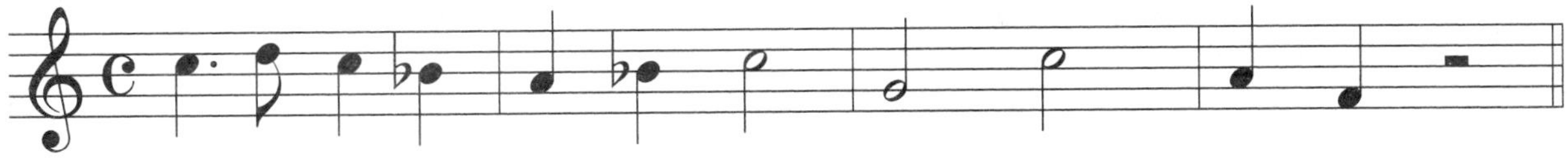

2. Transpose these melodies to the given key. Draw the transposition on the blank staff.

Melody 1: Key of G Major

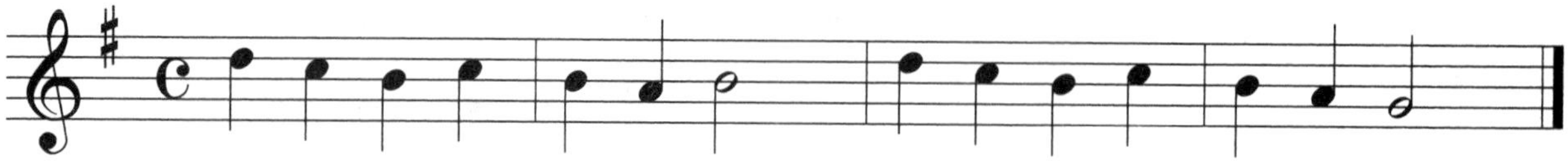

Transpose to C Major

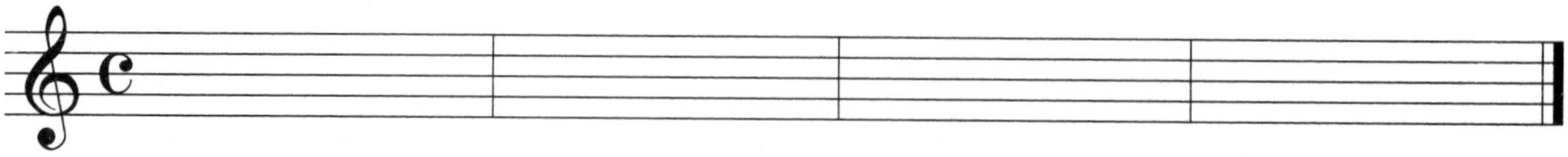

Melody 2: Key of C Major

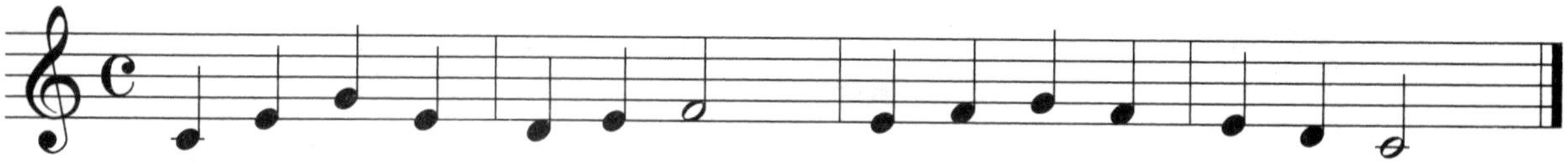

Transpose to G Major

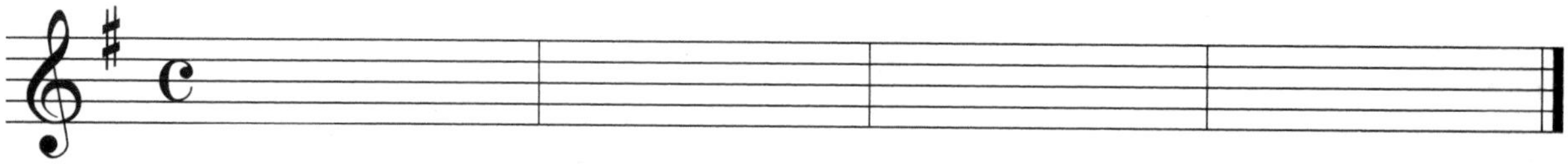

LESSON 15
MOTIVE; REPETITION, SEQUENCE, IMITATION

A **<u>MOTIVE</u>** (or **<u>motif</u>**) is a short musical idea upon which a composition is based. The motive and variations of the motive are repeated frequently throughout the music.

Minuet, L. 217 by Scarlatti uses this motive:

It is repeated, with variations, several times at the beginning and throughout the music:

<u>REPETITION</u> takes place when a motive is repeated immediately, exactly the way it was the first time it occurred and on the same note.

Sonatina in F by Beethoven uses repetition.

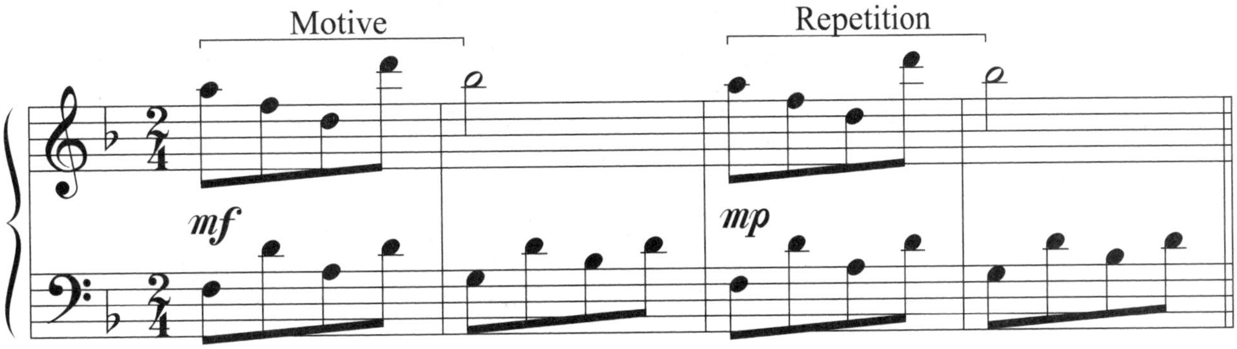

SEQUENCE occurs when the motive is repeated immediately on a different note, usually a 2nd or 3rd higher or lower.

Polonaise in g minor by J.S. Bach uses sequence.

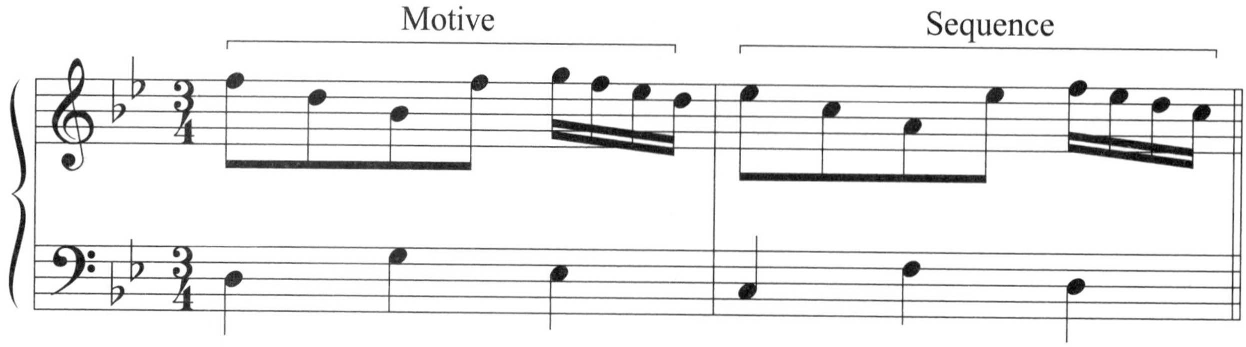

IMITATION occurs when the motive is repeated immediately in another voice, such as in the bass clef following a statement of the motive in the treble clef.

First Loss by Schumann uses imitation.

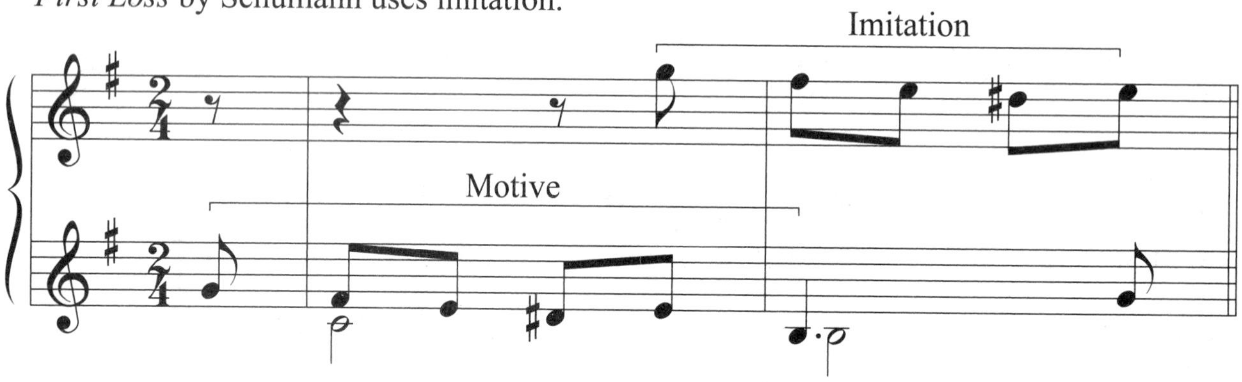

1. Circle the repetition, imitation, or sequence in each of the following phrases. Name the compositional technique. The first one is given.

a. From *Rondo Militaire* by Pleyel. Sequence

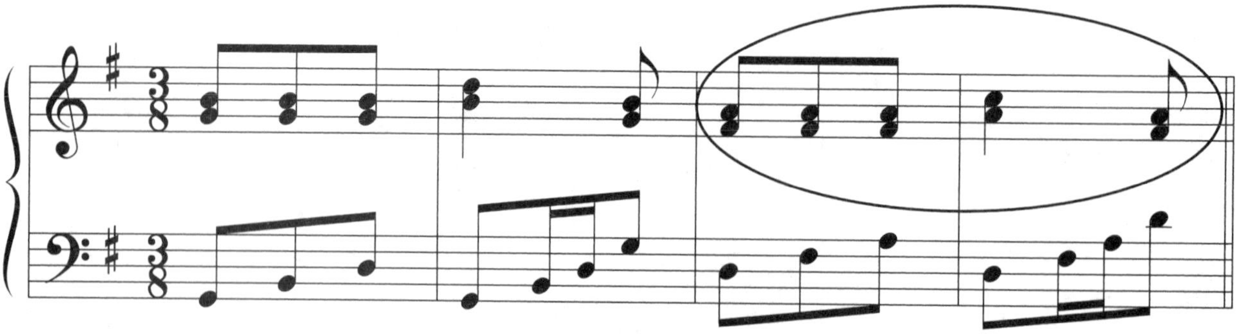

b. From *Sonatina, Op. 36, No. 2*, by Clementi. ____________________

c. From *Prelude* by Handel. ____________________

d. From *Hunting Song* by Schumann. ____________________

e. From *Polonaise in g minor* by J.S. Bach. ______________________

f. From *Short Prelude No. 4* by J.S. Bach. ______________________

LESSON 16
THE FOUR PERIODS OF MUSIC HISTORY

There are four periods of music history (dates are approximate):

BAROQUE: 1600-1750 (Bach, Handel, Scarlatti)

CLASSICAL: 1750-1830 (Mozart, Haydn, Clementi)

ROMANTIC: 1830-1900 (Tchaikovsky, Chopin, Schumann)

20th & 21st CENTURIES: 1900-Present (Kabalevsky, Bartók)

Currently, there is not a definitive name for stylistic periods of the 20th and 21st Centuries. Other names that are used include:

- Contemporary Period
- Modern
- Post Common Practice
- 20th Century (1900-1999) and Contemporary Period (2000-Present)

1. Write the names of the four periods of music history, their approximate dates, and composers of the period.

Historical Period	**Dates**	**Composers**
____________________	________	______________________________
____________________	________	______________________________
____________________	________	______________________________
____________________	________	______________________________

This page has purposely been left blank

REVIEW
LESSONS 12-16

1. Fill in the blanks.

2	=	_____ beats per measure, beat _____ is strongest
4	=	_______________ receives one beat
6	=	_____ beats per measure, beats _____ and _____ are strongest
8	=	_______________ receives one beat
3	=	3 beats per _______________, beat _____ is strongest
4	=	Quarter note receives _______________
9	=	9 beats per _______________
8	=	Eighth note receives _______________
4	=	_____ beats per measure, beats _____ and _____ are strongest
4	=	_______________ receives one beat
12	=	_____ beats per measure
8	=	_______________ receives one beat

2. Write counts between the clefs for these phrases. Draw accents on the strong beats.

a. From *Sailor's Song* by Grieg.

b. From *Hunting Song* by Schumann.

3. Define these words and symbols.

1. *andantino* ______________________________

2. *cantabile* ______________________________

3. *presto* ______________________________

4. *espressivo* ______________________________

5. *leggiero* ______________________________

6. *allegretto* ______________________________

7. -----*ino* ______________________________

8. *subito* ______________________________

9. -----*etto* ______________________________

10. 

____

11. parallel Major and minor ______________________________

12. articulation ______________________________

4. Circle the repetition, sequence, or imitation in each of the following phrases. Name the compositional technique.

a. From *Arabesque* by Burgmuller. ______________________________

b. From *Sonatina in C* by Gurlitt. ____________________________

c. From *Polonaise in g minor* by J.S. Bach. ____________________________

7. Name the four periods of music history and write their approximate dates.

PERIOD	**DATES**
____________________	____________________
____________________	____________________
____________________	____________________
____________________	____________________

8. Transpose this melody to the key of F Major. Draw the transposition on the blank staff.

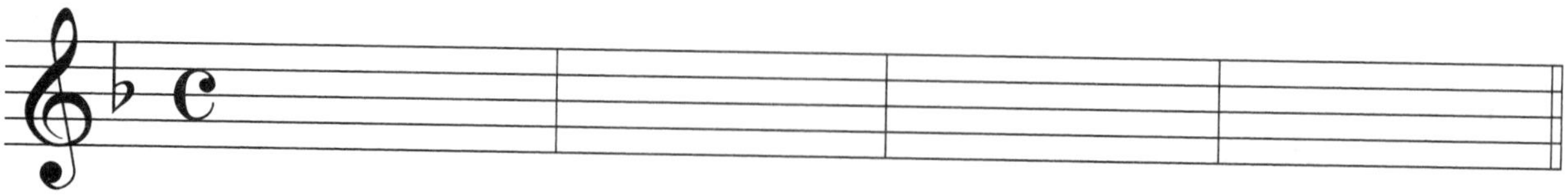

9. Add one rest to each measure to complete the following rhythm pattern.

10. Add one note to each measure to complete the following rhythm pattern.

11. Determine the time signature for each of the following rhythm patterns.

a. ____ 

b. ____ 

Score: ________

REVIEW TEST

Perfect Score = 98
Passing Score = 68

1. Name each of the following scales. For minor scales, include the form of minor (natural or harmonic). (4 points)

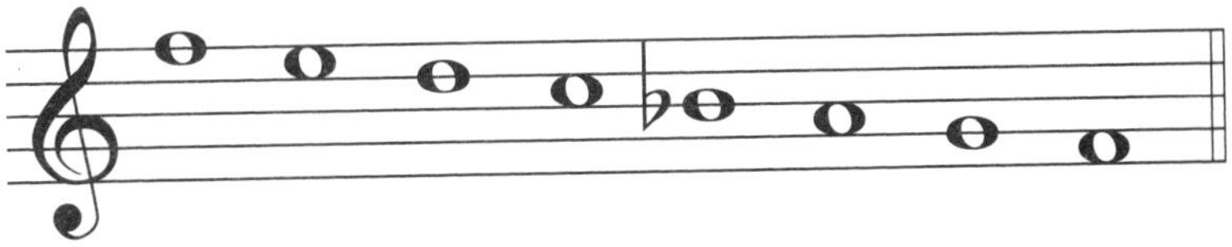

____ ______________

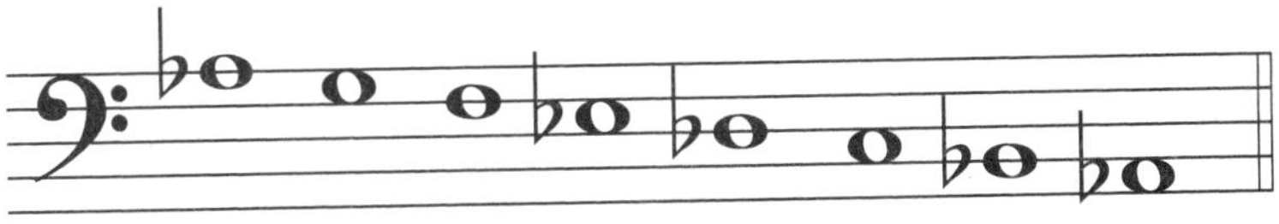

____ ______________

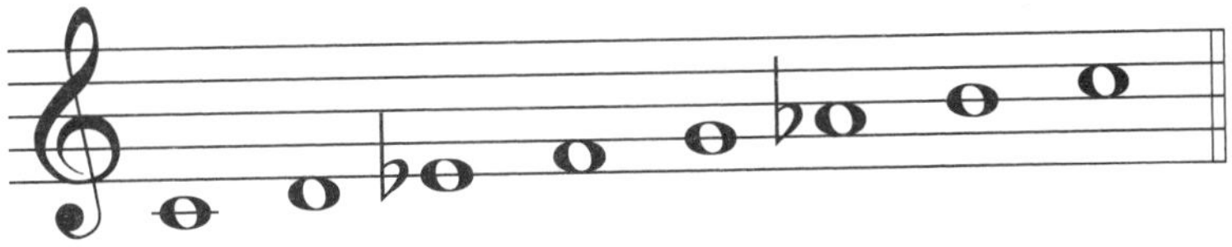

____ ______________

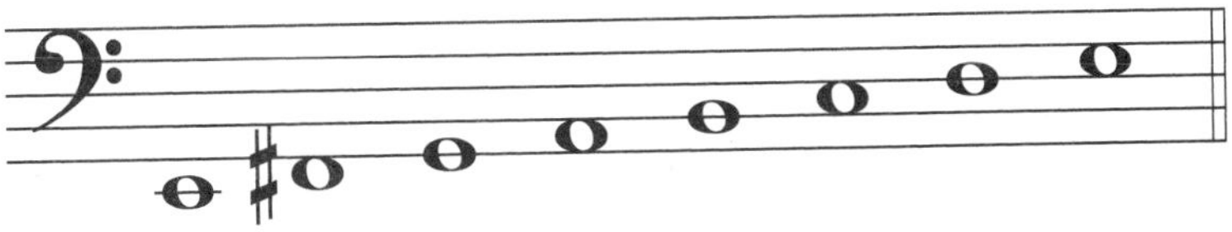

____ ______________

2. Draw the key signature for each of the following keys in both clefs. (4 points)

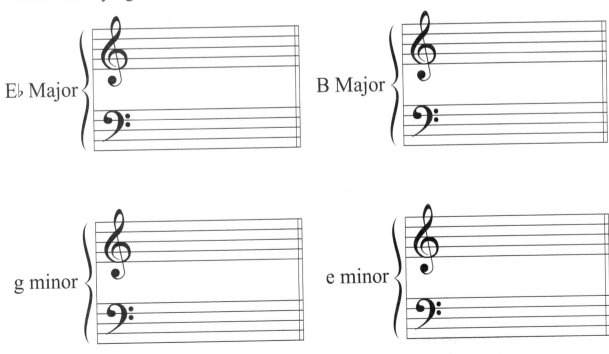

E♭ Major

B Major

g minor

e minor

3. a. Draw the Primary Triads for the key of a minor, harmonic form. Label the triads with Roman numerals. Do not use a key signature. Draw sharps or flats before the notes. Draw lines above and below the Roman numerals for Major chords. (6 points)

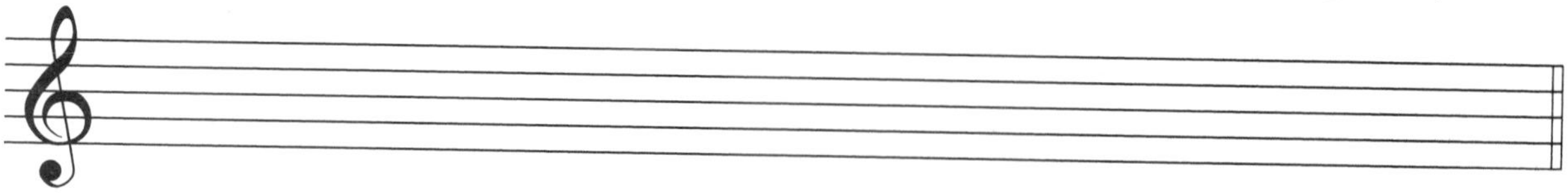

b. Draw the Secondary Triads for the key of F Major. Label the triads with Roman numerals. Do not use a key signature. Draw sharps or flats before the notes. Draw lines above and below the Roman numerals for Major chords. (8 points)

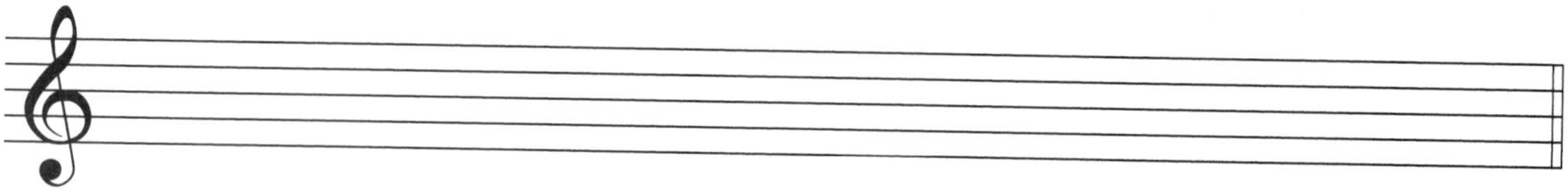

c. Draw the Primary and Secondary Triads for the key of G Major. Do not use a key signature. Draw sharps or flats before the notes. (8 points)

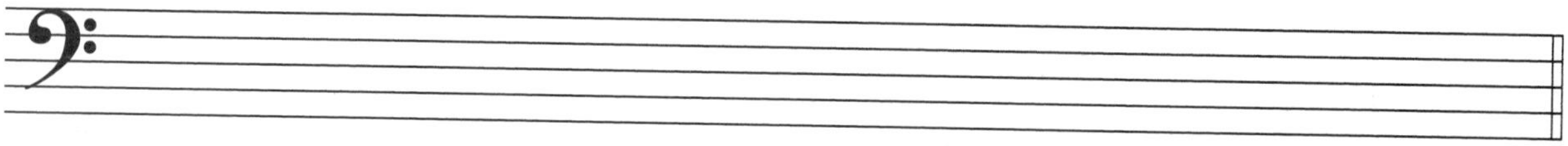

I ii iii IV V vi vii° I

4. The example above is from *Country Dance* by Mozart. Answer the following questions about the music. (6 points)

a. What is the key or tonality? ________ ________________

b. The notes in the bass clef of measure 2 outline a triad. Is this the tonic or dominant

triad? ______________________

c. This music is from the Classical Period. How is the trill in measure 1 to be played? (Circle the answer.)

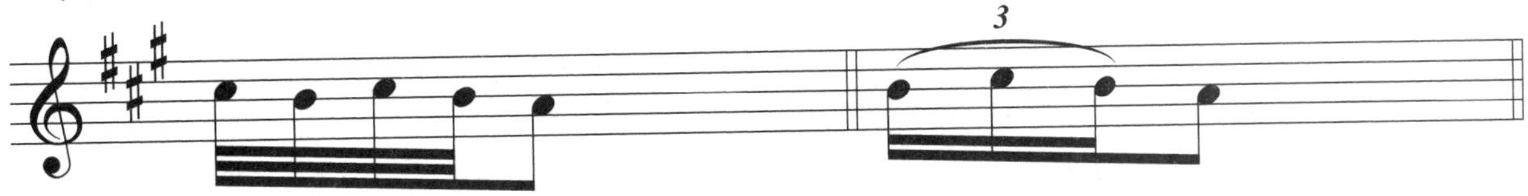

d. What is the time signature? _________________

e. Compare measures 1-2 with measure 3-4. Which compositional technique is used? (Circle the answer.)

Imitation　　　　　　Repetition

f. What is the meaning of *Moderato*? _________________________________

5. Answer these questions about the above music. (11 points)

a. What is the minor key or tonality? ______ ________________

b. Which form of minor is used? ____________________________

c. Does the example begin on the tonic note? ______________________

d. Name each circled interval with its quality and number. The first one is given.

Interval a. P4 b. ______ c. ______ d. _______ e. ______ f. _______

e. How many beats does the tie receive in measures 2-3? _________________

f. Which hand plays the melody? (Right or left) _________________________

g. Which beats will be strongest? ___________________________________

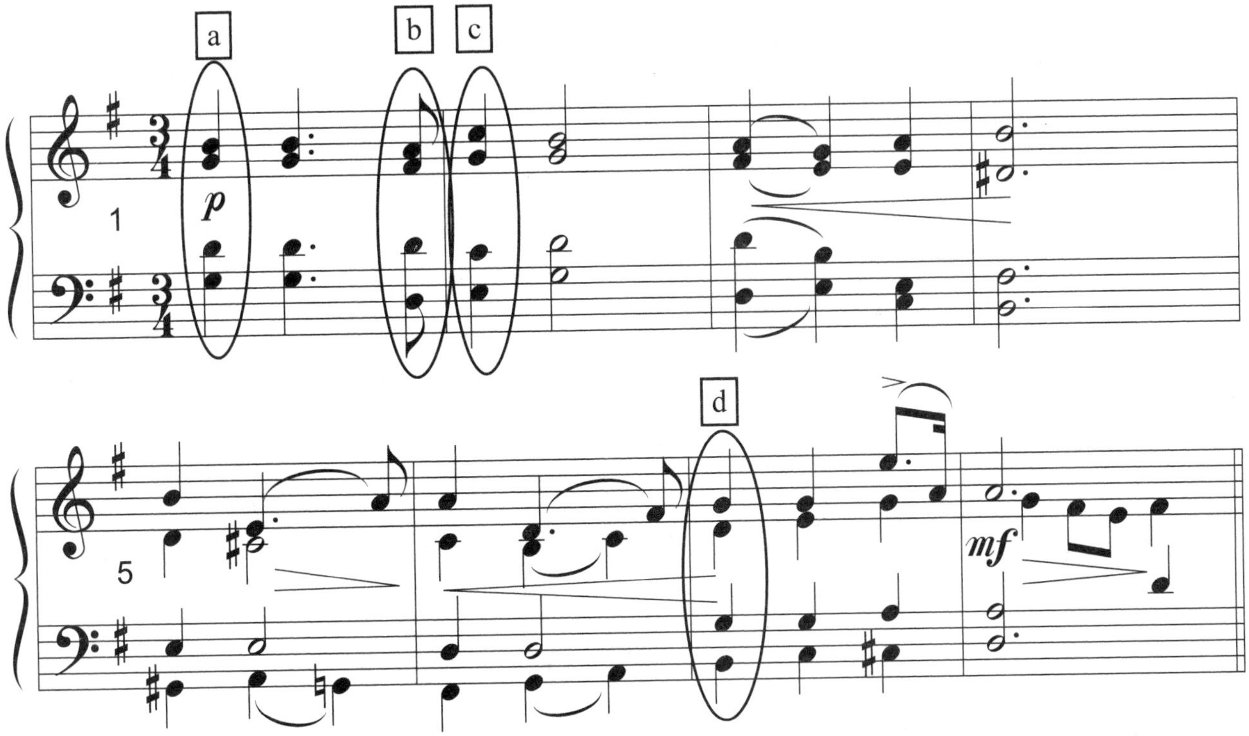

6. The example above is from *Morning Prayer* by Tchaikovsky. Answer the questions about the music. (16 points)

a. What is the key or tonality? ________ ____________________

b. Define the following terms used in the music.

p ______________________________________

(crescendo sign) ______________________________________

(decrescendo sign) ______________________________________

mf ______________________________________

c. Name each circled triad with its root, quality, Roman numeral, and inversion.

Triad a. ___G___ _______Major_______ ___I($^5_3$)___

Triad b. ______ ____________________ _________

Triad c. ______ ____________________ _________

Triad d. ______ ____________________ _________

d. What type of cadence occurs in measures 7-8? (Circle the answer.)

Plagal Half

e. Write counts between the clefs for measures 6-8. (Write the counts on the music.)

7. Match each of the following terms with its definition. (9 points)

a. parallel minor	_____	slightly slower than Allegro
b. *presto*	_____	lightly
c. *cantabile*	_____	suddenly
d. *espressivo*	_____	same letter name as Major
e. *leggiero*	_____	slightly faster than Andante
f. *andantino*	_____	very fast
g. *allegretto*	_____	in a singing style
h. *subito*	_____	ornament
i. trill	_____	expressively

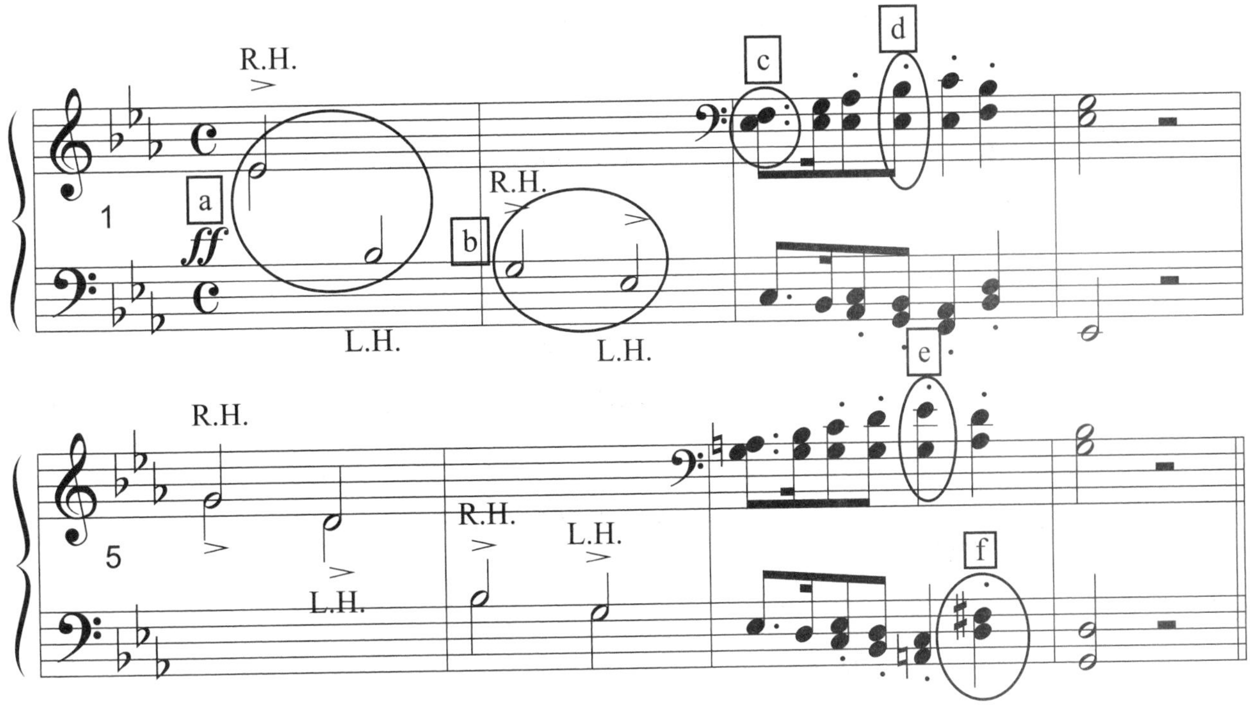

8. The above example is from *National Song* by Grieg. Answer the questions about the music. (15 points)

a. What is the key or tonality of measures 1-4? ________ ________________

b. What is the key of measures 5-8? ________ ________________

c. Name each circled interval with its quality and number. The first one is given.

Interval a. __P4__ b. ______ c. ______ d. ______ e. ______ f. ______

d. Name each of the following triads with its root, quality, and inversion.

	ROOT	**QUALITY**	**INVERSION**
Beat 4, measure 3:	________	____________	______________
Beat 1, measure 4:	________	____________	______________

e. The triads above make a V-I cadence. What is the name for this? (Circle the answer.)

Half   Authentic

f. Write the counts for measures 3-4. (Write the counts on the music.)

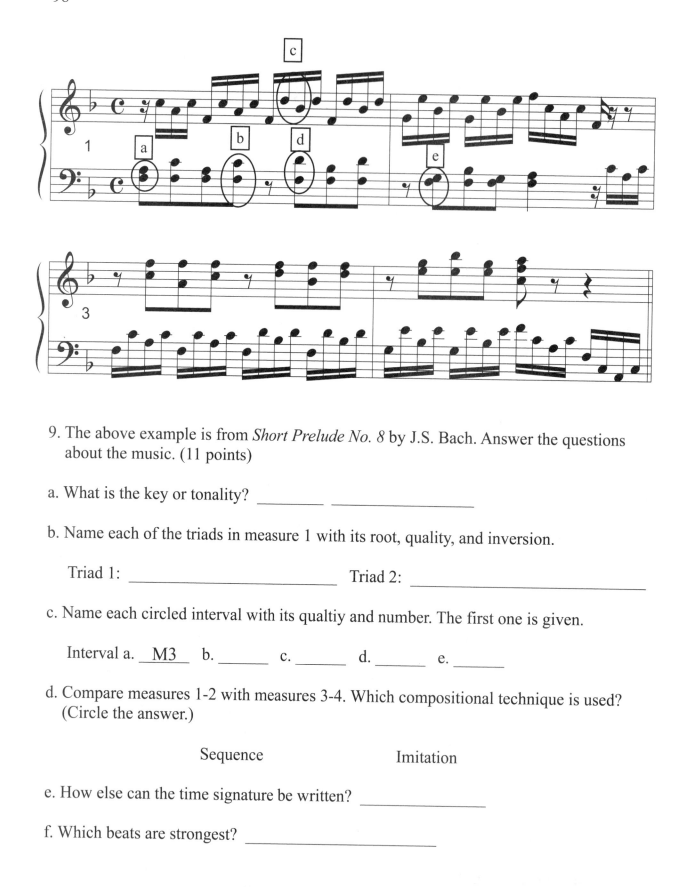

9. The above example is from *Short Prelude No. 8* by J.S. Bach. Answer the questions about the music. (11 points)

a. What is the key or tonality? ________ __________________

b. Name each of the triads in measure 1 with its root, quality, and inversion.

Triad 1: __________________________ Triad 2: ____________________________

c. Name each circled interval with its qualtiy and number. The first one is given.

Interval a. __M3__ b. ______ c. ______ d. ______ e. ______

d. Compare measures 1-2 with measures 3-4. Which compositional technique is used? (Circle the answer.)

Sequence Imitation

e. How else can the time signature be written? ________________

f. Which beats are strongest? ________________________

REFERENCES

Apel, Willi. *Harvard Dictionary of Music, Second Edition.* Cambridge, Massachusetts: Belknap Press of Harvard University Press, 1972.

Arnold, Denis, ed. *The New Oxford Companion to Music, Volumes 1 and 2.* New York: Oxford University Press, 1983.

Music Teachers' Association of California.® *Certificate of Merit® Piano Syllabus, 1992 Edition.* San Francisco: Music Teachers' Association of California, 1992.

Music Teachers' Association of California.® *Certificate of Merit® Piano Syllabus, 1997 Edition.* Ontario, Canada: The Frederick Harris Music Company, Limited, 1997.

Music Teachers' Association of California.® *Certificate of Merit® Piano Syllabus, 2007 Edition..* San Francisco: Music Teachers' Association of California, 2007.

Music Teachers' Association of California.® *Certificate of Merit® Piano Syllabus, 2012 Edition.* San Francisco: Music Teachers' Association of California, 2012.

Sadie, Stanley, ed. *The New Grove Dictionary of Music and Musicians.* Washington, D.C.: Grove's Dictionaries of Music Inc., 1980.